Lodges Examined by the Bible

Is It a Sin for a Christian to Have Membership in Secret Orders?

By JOHN R. RICE

ISBN 0-87398-510-9

SWORD of the LORD
PUBLISHERS
P.O.BOX 1099, MURFREESBORO, TN 37133

Printed in U.S.A.

Table of Contents

CHAPTER I

Why I Write Against Lodges

In the United States there are about eight hundred different secret societies, and nearly half of the adult men and women of the United States are affiliated with them, according to the Rev. James Putt, Th.M., in the scholarly pamphlet *Masonry*. He quotes the Grand Lodge Bulletin of Iowa that for 1936 there were 2,665,511 Masons. Masonry is the oldest secret order, the largest, and the parent of the others.

Multitudes of the most influential people are members of secret orders. The membership includes hosts of church members and many preachers. Many active church workers are proud to wear the lodge ring or pin. A good many preachers leave the active ministry to become lodge lecturers. Lodges are called on to lay the cornerstones for new church buildings, and preachers frequently announce special sermons to groups of lodge members. A great many men that I know and love, including preachers, are members of lodges. My own father was very active as a Mason and an Odd Fellow. The lodges claim to be centers of morality, claim to subdue the passions of men, claim to give great light on spiritual things, and by many are claimed to be great aids to Christianity. The lodges themselves often profess to show the way to Heaven. They speak much about God, have Bibles as lodge furniture, have priests, chaplains, Worshipful Masters; their buildings are often called temples. And now we are to examine the lodges in the light of the Bible, the Word of God. And we ask the question, "Is it a sin for a Christian to have membership in secret orders?"

The answer is that the lodges in general are unchristian and anti-christian institutions, institutions that teach a pagan false religion, not Christianity; institutions where the saved and the lost mingle as brethren; where Christians, Jews, Mohammedans and Hindus are all on the same plane; where men call on God but do not come in the name of Christ; where the Scriptures are mutilated by omitting Christ's name; where horrible, blood-curdling, unchristian oaths are required; institutions opposed to the Christian attitude, grieving the Spirit of God and violating the plain command of the Bible to swear not at all. All these things we will prove in these brief chapters, prove so thoroughly that honest, humble Christian men and women who are willing to take the Word of God as a binding authority, and willing to investigate the evidence

4

and follow the leading of the Holy Spirit, will be thoroughly convinced.

For a child of God to be a member of a lodge, a secret order, is a sin. It is the sin of spiritual adultery when the children of light yoke up with the children of darkness and when the temples of God are turned over to idol worship. The sin of a Christian in the lodge is the sin of Lot in Sodom, calling the Sodomites *brethren*. It is the sin of Solomon in marrying many strange, heathen wives and then following them in idolatrous worship. It is the sin of Peter, warming by the Devil's fire and denying his Lord.

If my words seem strong, then the evidence will be stronger. Here is a matter upon which honest Christians, earnestly seeking to know the will of God, can find with certainty what they ought to do. If you investigate this matter as thousands of other Christians have done, seeking only to follow the Word of God and to please Christ Jesus our Lord and Saviour, then you will come to the same conclusion that thousands of others have reached in this matter and will leave lodges and secret orders as places where no child of God ought to be found.

Let it be understood that I am discussing the lodges themselves and not lodge *members.* I know many lodge members for whom I have great respect and tender love. I know many who are real Christians, born again and sincere lovers of the Lord Jesus Christ. But mark you, the lodges did not make them Christians. Rather, lodges may lead Christians to sin. I say the plain, sharp facts I shall give are about certain institutions, institutions which are contrary to the Bible and hurtful for Christians, institutions that dishonor Christ and the Bible. Good men and women in these institutions are often deceived as to the character of the organizations to which they belong. *If I can, I will help such people, and I certainly mean no unkindness toward them.* My own father was a very ardent and active Mason and an Odd Fellow. I revere his name. He is now in Heaven. Of his sincerity I have no doubt. Many other Christians, equally sincere, have been trapped into yoking up with unbelievers in secret orders. Most respectfully and kindly and lovingly I seek to show them their mistake and to tell the truth and prove it concerning the institutions of which they are members.

Some will be offended at the plain speech here used. Some who love the lodges better than the church of Jesus Christ will not see the harm in yoking up with unbelievers. Some who have taken the claims of secret orders at face value will be surprised at things I will tell about the lodges and will find it hard to believe that all I say is so. To such I promise faithfully that I will give evidence and tell where to find plenty more to prove every statement and implication I make. Some, perhaps, who have sworn bloody oaths to "ever conceal and never reveal" the so-called secrets of their lodge, will even deny the truth because the oath they took, they think binds them to lie, if necessary, to conceal the truth. Yet the so-called secrets are not secret at all but are printed for all who really want to find out the truth. All I ask is that every reader prayerfully study the facts and weigh the Word of God on the question with a surrendered heart, and then follow the plain leading of the Holy Spirit.

Since Masonry is the oldest and largest secret order, and since the other large secret orders are largely patterned after Masonry, it will be necessary in many, many cases to use Masonry as an example. Besides, there is vastly more literature on Masonry. And since, too, I was initiated into a Masonic lodge as Entered Apprentice, and since my father was an active and ardent Mason, I was led to make a detailed study through a course of many years concerning Masonry. Hence what I shall say will deal largely with Masonry. However, in general principles the lodges are much the same; and if it is a sin for a Christian to be a member of the Masonic fraternity, then it is not hard to see that it would be equally wrong to yoke up with unbelievers in other lodges.

It was in the summer of 1921, I believe, when, influenced by many friends, I went to the lodge to be made a Mason. A preacher friend said, "To be a Mason will give you a lot more influence. You can reach many men through your Masonic connections whom you could not otherwise reach. And it is a great factor in the safety of you and your family to be a Mason."

My father said that he, of course, could not ask me to become a Mason, but that nevertheless it would be a great help to me in my work as a preacher. All I had ever heard about the secret orders was good, or nearly all. Many preachers whom I had known and loved and respected were Masons. I was told that Solomon, John the Baptist, the Apostle John, and other Bible characters were Masons and that this ancient fraternity held in trust many great spiritual truths that the rest of the world did not have. Just previously I had surrendered to preach the gospel of Christ, and I was anxious to have all the help I could have in winning men. So I presented myself for membership.

But the lodge was a great disillusionment to me. A man whom I knew as a practical infidel, who laughed at the inspiration of the Bible and mocked the idea of Christ being the divine Son of God, a rationalist who despised the churches, I found to be the most active and prominent member of the lodge! He stood at my father's elbow as the work of the degree progressed, prompting him. This was a notoriously profane man whom I had heard take God's name in vain, yet he was the lodge brother and bosom companion of my father, who before his lodge days had been an active preacher of the gospel! Others who made no pretense to being children of God were in the lodge room. Without loving Christ or having trusted Him for salvation, they spoke familiarly of God and were on the same basis as earnest Christians and preachers of the gospel.

When I was asked to repeat after my father words of the Apprentice's oath, I began and then stopped. I had no idea that such an oath was a part of Masonry, and I did not want to proceed. My father and others told me that there was nothing in the oath nor in Masonry that would be offensive to God or my conscience. I continued. But I was shocked, and the more I thought of it the more shocked I was at the words I had spoken. When I was presented with the white apron and told that I was to be buried in it and that at my funeral Masons should have charge and Masonry exalted, my heart cried out that if I should die I wanted a simple gospel sermon and I wanted sinners to hear about the blood of Christ, I wanted an invitation given! And so I went away that night, grieved and shocked. The Holy Spirit within me seemed offended. I never went back to the lodge. After some months' time, I came to the conclusion that I had sinned in going there and taking part in such language and ceremonies and in such company. I asked God to forgive me and promised Him never to take up the work, although good friends had volunteered to pay the cost of my first three degrees. (Later that offer was made again.)

At that time I had never read a line of intelligent criticism of the lodges, as far as I can remember. I was not familiar with the Bible and did not bring to mind at that time a single Scripture on the question. I simply knew that I, a young preacher of the gospel on fire for souls and earnestly seeking to please God in every detail of my life and vowing to follow the leading of the Holy Spirit within me, was out of place in the lodges. The Holy Spirit told me that was no place for me. Later I learned that multiplied thousands of other Christians had had the same experience that I had had. Later, as I read the Bible, I found abundant Scripture commanding a Christian to be free from anything like the lodges.

CHAPTER II

Plain-as-Day Scriptures Forbidding Lodge Membership for Christians

Here are Scriptures that cannot be misunderstood nor explained away. Will you be honest with God and His Word before you lay this book down?

I. SCRIPTURES FORBIDDING CHRISTIANS TO YOKE UP WITH UNBELIEVERS IN LODGES OR TO HAVE FELLOWSHIP AND BROTHERHOOD WITH UNCONVERTED MEN:

1. Second Corinthians 6:14-18:

"Be ye not unequally yoked together with unbelievers: for what fellowship hath righteousness with unrighteousness? and what communion hath light with darkness? And what concord hath Christ with Belial? Or what part hath he that believeth with an infidel? And what agreement hath the temple of God with idols? for ye are the temple of the living God; as God hath said, I will dwell in them, and walk in them; and I will be their God, and they shall be my people. Wherefore come out from among them, and be ye separate, saith the Lord, and touch not the unclean thing; and I will receive you, And will be a Father unto you, and ye shall be my sons and daughters, saith the Lord Almighty."

Notice that a Christian is plainly forbidden to have "fellowship," "communion," "concord," "part," or "agreement," with those who do not have saving faith. But in all the lodges one is yoked up by binding oaths with people who are already condemned because they do not believe in Jesus Christ as Saviour.

2. Psalm 1:1:

"Blessed is the man that walketh not in the counsel of the ungodly, nor standeth in the way of sinners, nor sitteth in the seat of the scornful."

God's blessed man does not walk, nor stand, nor sit, with the ungodly (unconverted), nor sinners (those who live in sin), nor the scornful (those who doubt the Bible, the deity of Christ, salvation by blood, etc.). This verse could not fit any man in membership and fellowship and attendance on lodges.

3. Ephesians 5:11, 12:

"And have no fellowship with the unfruitful works of darkness, but rather reprove them. For it is a shame even to speak of those things which are done of them in secret."

The works of the lodges are unfruitful, that is, their work is not to get sinners saved. They are works of darkness, that is, works of secrecy and hidden things. But God commands, 'have no fellowship with them, but rather reprove them.'

4. Matthew 12:48-50:

"But he answered and said unto him that told him, Who is my mother? and who are my brethren? And he stretched forth his hand toward his disciples, and said, Behold my mother and my brethren! For whosoever shall do the will of my Father which is in heaven, the same is my brother, and sister, and mother."

All lodges bind their members by oath to regard lodge members as their brothers or sisters and to favor lodge members above others. But Jesus says that His brothers and sisters are only those who do the will of the Father, Christians. It is wrong to call unconverted people "brethren" or to be bound closer to them than with Christians.

5. Second John 9-11:

"Whosoever transgresseth, and abideth not in the doctrine of Christ, hath not God. He that abideth in the doctrine of Christ, he hath both the Father and the Son. If there come any unto you, and bring not this doctrine, receive him not into your house, neither bid him God speed: For he that biddeth him God speed is partaker of his evil deeds."

The lodges do not pray in the name of Christ; they teach salvation without Christ, by character and good works, and recognize the god of Mohammedans or of other heathen religions as equal with the true God. Lodges, when they quote Scriptures, omit the name of Jesus Christ. Christians are forbidden to bid them God speed in their evil work. All Christians in the lodges bid God speed to their Christ rejection and false doctrine.

II. CONCERNING SECRECY OF THE LODGES:

1. John 18:20:

"Jesus answered him, I spake openly to the world; I ever taught in the synagogue, and in the temple, whither the Jews always resort; and in secret have I said nothing."

Jesus had nothing to do with secret doctrines or rites or oaths. Should you?

2. Matthew 10:26, 27:

"Fear them not therefore: for there is nothing covered, that shall not be revealed; and hid, that shall not be known. What I tell you in darkness, that speak ye in light: and what ye hear in the ear, that preach ye upon the housetops."

Secret things will all be published, and Christians are expressly commanded to preach upon the housetops what they hear in the ear. But lodge oaths contradict the command of Christ.

3. Ephesians 5:11, 12:

"And have no fellowship with the unfruitful works of darkness, but rather reprove them. For it is a shame even to speak of those things which are done of them in secret."

The works of darkness (secrecy) are unfruitful and shameful. Christians should have no fellowship with them but should reprove them, says God's Word.

III. CONCERNING THE OATHS OF THE LODGES:

1. Matthew 5:34-37:

"But I say unto you, Swear not at all; neither by heaven; for it is God's throne: Nor by the earth; for it is his footstool: neither by Jerusalem; for it is the city of the great King. Neither shalt thou swear by thy head, because thou canst not make one hair white or black. But let your communication be, Yea, yea; Nay, nay: for whatsoever is more than these cometh of evil."

"Swear not at all," Christian, Jesus said. No lodge member in the world has kept this command.

2. James 5:12:

"But above all things, my brethren, swear not, neither by heaven, neither by the earth, neither by any other oath: but let your yea be yea; and your nay, nay; lest ye fall into condemnation."

Notice that the command "Swear not" is "above all things, my brethren." Notice He commands, ". . . neither by any other oath." Any oath at all is a sin. Every lodge member violates this plain command in every degree he takes.

3. Exodus 20:7:

"Thou shalt not take the name of the Lord thy God in vain; for the Lord will not hold him guiltless that taketh his name in vain."

The name of God is used repeatedly in lodge ritual, and used in insincere forms, even by unconverted men. Lodge members break this one of the Ten Commandments repeatedly. Lodge members who would keep their oaths would sometimes be murderers, since many oaths involve bloodshed. Christians certainly sin when they swear and when they take God's name in vain in lodges.

4. Leviticus 5:4-6:

"Or if a soul swear, pronouncing with his lips to do evil, or to do good, whatsoever it be that a man shall pronounce with an oath, and it be hid from him; when he knoweth of it, then he shall be guilty in one of these. And it shall be, when he shall be guilty in one of these things, that he shall confess that he hath sinned in that thing: And he shall bring his trespass-offering unto the Lord for his sin which he hath sinned, a female from the flock, a lamb or a kid of the goats, for a sin-offering; and the priest shall make an atonement for him concerning his sin."

If you took a lodge oath and then later found it was a sin, you should confess that you have sinned in this matter and renounce it. God does not hold you to a wicked oath but counts it a sin which you should confess and forsake. Lodge oaths are not binding on Christians who see and confess the sin and renounce them.

These Scriptures will be discussed further in succeeding chapters.

CHAPTER III

Christians Sin by Yoking Up With Unbelievers in Lodges

The following passage of Scripture should convince every child of God of the sin in belonging to lodges or secret orders:

"Be ye not unequally yoked together with unbelievers: for what fellowship hath righteousness with unrighteousness? and what communion hath light with darkness? And what concord hath Christ with Belial? or what part hath he that believeth with an infidel? And what agreement hath the temple of God with idols? for ye are the temple of the living God; as God hath said, I will dwell in them, and walk in them; and I will be their God, and they shall be my people. Wherefore come out from among them, and be ye separate, saith the Lord, and touch not the unclean thing; and I will receive you, And will be a Father unto you, and ye shall be my sons and daughters, saith the Lord Almighty."—II Cor. 6:14-18.

It is wrong for believers to be yoked with unbelievers, and impossible for righteousness to have fellowship with unrighteousness, for light to have communion with darkness, for Christ to have concord with Belial, and out of order for believers to have part with infidels. It is wrong for the temple of God to have agreement with idols, and the people of God are plainly commanded, "Wherefore come out from among them, and be ye separate."

THE IRONCLAD, OATH-BOUND YOKE OF LODGE MEMBERSHIP

Since God forbids Christians to be yoked with unbelievers, then does lodge membership involve such a yoke as the Scripture forbids? Most certainly it does! The lodge yoke is intended to be as binding as any relationship on earth. It is not to be compared with membership in a labor union nor in a banker's association or a service club, though even these are sometimes of a nature that spiritually-minded Christians cannot conscientiously belong to them. But consider how binding is the forbidden yoke of lodge membership.

First, the lodge oath presumes to be even more sacred than the marriage vow. By solemn and frightful oath the Mason swears that he will ever conceal and never reveal to anyone not proven to be a Mason the secrets and doings of Masonry. From the wife that God says is his own flesh, the wife of his bosom, the mother of his children, the Mason is sworn to conceal the facts about what he does and says, who are his companions, and what are the teachings of the lodge. The wife may help to make and save the money that he spends for expensive Masonic degrees, yet the things purchased must be kept secret from her. The husband may stay out until the late hours of the night while the wife remains alone, yet he is sworn not to explain to her what took place that kept him so long. Such a yoke is unreasonable for any man to take upon himself, and it is positively forbidden a child of God.

The lodge yoke is so binding that it presumes to supersede the duty of a man to his church, to fellow Christians, or even to his pastor. The union of Christians as they meet together in God's name is so precious that Jesus Himself promises, "For where two or three are gathered together in my name, there am I in the midst of them" (Matt. 18:20). Christians are commanded, "Bear ye one another's burdens, and so fulfill the law of Christ" (Gal. 6:2). Christians are commanded of God to "rejoice with them that do rejoice, and weep with them that weep" (Rom. 12:15). Yet a Christian lodge member is solemnly sworn with frightful penalties not to discuss the so-called secrets of his order with the best Christian brother he has in the world if that one be not able to prove himself a brother in the lodge. No church ever presumes to bind its members under such a galling yoke as that which a Christian must take on himself with unbelievers when he joins the lodge.

In time of sickness or in the presence of death, in time of temptation or of holy fellowship with God, a Mason is sworn under threat of death not to discuss the so-called secrets of his lodge with even his pastor, the shepherd whom God has placed over his soul and commanded him to obey; that is, unless the pastor is a member of the same lodge! And that galling yoke that shuts out wife or son or brother Christian, or even the godly pastor, and binds one in for life with ungodly men, with Christ-rejecters—that is the yoke that Christians take in joining lodges.

The Mason swears to show partiality to Masons over those not Masons and binds himself to show a preference to his lodge "brother" that he is not to show to his Christian brother in Christ if that Christian brother be not a Mason. In politics, honest Masons must prefer lodge members, other things being equal. The oath is so binding that in some degrees of Masonry, Masons are sworn to help deliver fellow Masons from any kind of trouble, "murder and treason excepted." The oath plainly has in mind the delivery of a criminal from punishment for his crime since it plainly says, "murder and treason excepted." Crimes of rape, theft, arson—Masons are sworn to help deliver Masons from punishment brought on by such crimes. And in the Royal Arch Degree, the oath changes, and murder and treason are not excepted. That is, advanced Masons are sworn to help one another out of their troubles and that without exception. So the yoke of Masonry is so binding that it presumes to be stronger than a man's citizenship, his duty to the law of the land. And that is not strange. If it would come between a man and his wife, between a Christian and his pastor, then the lodge would not blush to come between a citizen and his duty to his government.

Remember that lodge members are bound also by the hope of gain. They put hundreds of dollars into membership fees and degrees, and in return they expect to get help in time of sickness or support in old age. Particularly they expect help for the widow and orphan children should the head of the family die. Self-interest is strong and ties one all the more tightly into the organization which includes many ungodly and unregenerate men or women.

And last of all, a terrible threat hangs over the head of every lodge member who does not remain true to his lodge. The lodge member does not want his tongue torn out and buried in the sands of the sea at low tide where the tide ebbs and flows twice in twenty-four hours. He does not want his left breast cut open and his heart taken out and fed to wild beasts and birds of prey. He does not want his skull cleft off and his brain exposed to the burning sun. He does not want his body cut in two, half to the north and half to the south, and his bowels burned to ashes in the midst. He does not want a spear or a sharp instrument thrust into his side, the mark of the cross in his death. *And he is sworn to expect such penalties if he is untrue to his vows as a Mason.* Such oaths, growing increasingly violent, mark the various degrees of Masonry. And suppose that he thinks these penalties would not be enforced. Still he does not want to face the hatred and malice that they represent. He does not want to be persecuted to the end of his days as a vagabond and a traitor, as he knows that men solemnly swear to do to those who are untrue to Masonic obligations.

Surely no intelligent man or woman could say that the lodge yoke is not a terribly binding one and the kind expressly forbidden in the Bible when it commands, "Be ye not unequally yoked together with unbelievers" (II Cor. 6:14).

Lodge Membership Binds Christians With Unbelievers

The Scripture says, "Be ye not unequally yoked together with unbelievers," and the lodges are full of unbelievers.

Of course we mean unbelievers in the Bible sense. Those who have not received Christ as Saviour and Lord and do not believe on Him with dependent faith, trusting Him alone for a new heart and everlasting life, are called unbelievers in the Bible. And it is with these that God forbids a Christian to be yoked. John 3:18 says, "He that believeth on him is not condemned: but he that believeth not is condemned already, because he hath not believed in the name of the only begotten Son of God." You see that a believer in the Bible is one who has saving faith in Christ, and an unbeliever is one who rejects Christ and does not trust Him for salvation, has not been born again through faith in Christ. In literally dozens of Scriptures that is made clear. For instance, John 3:36 says, "He that believeth on the Son hath everlasting life: and he that believeth not the Son shall not see life; but the wrath of God abideth on him." An unbeliever is one who does not have a saving faith in Jesus Christ, has not personally received Him into the heart by faith. Now certainly no one can deny that the lodges include multitudes of unconverted people, people who are unbelievers in the sense that they have never received Christ as a personal Saviour, have never received everlasting life through being born again by faith.

Occasionally, in self defense, a Christian who has joined unbelievers in the lodges will say that no one can be a true Mason or a true Odd Fellow without being a Christian. But the facts in the case are that the teachings of the lodges and the statements of high authorities in the lodges all prove that untrue. Neither Masons nor Odd Fellows nor any other secret order with which I am familiar requires one to accept Christ as Saviour. Both Masons and Odd Fellows require one to believe that there is a Supreme Being, and nothing more than that. Jews, who believe that Christ was only the bastard son of a Jewish harlot, are welcomed in the lodges and are not embarrassed. They believe there is a God, and that is enough. Mohammedans, who say that Allah is the one God and Mohammed is his prophet, can be received and are received in the largest secret orders as regular members. And certainly, then, the lodges make no bones about receiving ordinary men who believe there is a Supreme Being but who are Christ-rejecters and have never received Christ as Saviour. The lodges have multitudes of unbelievers, and any Christian who joins a secret order commits the horrible sin of yoking up with unbelievers, which is specifically forbidden by the Word of God.

When I entered the Masonic lodge room for the first time, I was shocked to find that a blasphemer, a profane swearer, one who plainly told me that he did not believe the miracles of the Bible and one who did not accept Christ as the virgin-born Son of God nor believe in Him as Saviour, was the most prominent man in the lodge. I found that many other wicked and unconverted men were members of the lodge along with church members and some preachers.

The principal leaders among high and active lodge members are usually unbelievers. Dr. Joseph Fort Newton, a modernist who denies the inspiration of the Bible, the deity of Christ, the atoning power of the blood of Christ, the need for a new birth, and every fundamental of the Christian faith, is a principal writer for Masons. In the Bible sense, he is an unbeliever. I read many, many copies of the *New Age Magazine* and found many startling statements of rationalism and unbelief. One writer, for instance, high in Masonic circles, said that the body of Jesus decayed in the grave and that now somewhere on a hillside in Judaea the very dust that was in the body of Christ yet remained. He did not believe in the resurrection of Christ nor His deity and had not trusted Him as a divine Saviour, God's sacrifice for sin. I have repeatedly talked to active and advanced Masons who insisted on salvation by character and knew nothing of salvation by the blood. And no one is ever a child of God until he trusts in the atoning blood of Christ. In the Bible sense, everyone is an unbeliever who does not accept Christ as the Lamb of God, depend upon Him for salvation, a new heart, everlasting life.

It must become obvious to the careful observer that because of the dances, the horseplay, and the drinking which so often attend the Shrine meetings, these Masonic meetings must be dominated by unconverted men. The De Molay dances, though opened with prayer, sometimes by preachers, yet surely are an indication that multitudes of these lodge members are unbelievers and do not know Christ as Saviour and Lord.

The lodges, then, have many unbelievers and many ungodly people and every child of God who is a lodge member is thereby yoked up with unbelievers.

WHY THIS YOKE WITH UNBELIEVERS IS A HORRIBLE SIN

We have proven that one who joins the lodge is under a binding, galling, ironclad, oath-bound yoke. We have shown how this yoke is with unbelievers in the Bible sense. Now let us see why it is such a wicked sin for a Christian to yoke up with unbelievers in the lodges.

"Wherefore come out from among them, and be ye separate, saith the Lord," is the command of II Corinthians 6:17 after God said, "Be ye not unequally yoked together with unbelievers." This teaching that a child of God should be separate, not joining in with the wicked, the ungodly and unbelievers, is one of the clearest in the Bible. In the ceremonial law which God gave to the Jews, He gave very clear spiritual lessons for us. Deuteronomy 22:9-11 says:

"Thou shalt not sow thy vineyard with divers seeds: lest the fruit of thy seed which thou hast sown, and the fruit of thy vineyard, be defiled. Thou shalt not plow with an ox and an ass together. Thou shalt not wear a garment of divers sorts, as of woollen and linen together."

When the Jewish boy was eight days old, he was marked with circumcision to remind him all his life he was of a separate people, set apart for the Lord. When a Jew sat down at the table, he was reminded that he must watch what he ate and not eat as did Gentiles. When a Jew put on his shirt, he could not put on a garment of mixed cloth as linen and wool. That was a spiritual lesson to him, as to us, that he was not to mix with idolaters and unbelievers. When an Israelitish farmer hitched up his team, he had to remember not to plow with an ox and an ass together. That was a reminder to him and to us that God does not want His people to be mixed in with unbelievers. When a Jew sowed his vineyard, he had to remember that he could not sow mixed seed in the same field. The spiritual lesson God had for him is still good for us, that one who believes in God must not mix with unbelievers. The letter of the ceremonial law is not for us, but surely the spiritual lessons are still true. We should be separate, a peculiar people for God, and should not yoke up with unbelievers.

The terrible wickedness which preceded and caused the flood was, as some believe, the result of the godly seed of Seth, called "sons of God," intermarrying with the unsaved women, "daughters of men" (Gen. 6:1, 2). Read also down to verse 7 and see that this intermarriage caused the wickedness which compelled God to destroy the race by the flood.

Solomon sinned against God in mixing with unbelievers. First Kings 11:4, 5 tells us:

"For it came to pass, when Solomon was old, that his wives turned away his heart after other gods: and his heart was not perfect with the Lord his God, as was the heart of David his father. For Solomon went after Ashtoreth the goddess of the Zidonians, and after Milcom the abomination of the Ammonites."

If it was a sin for Solomon to marry wives of heathen religions, and if Solomon was led away after these idol gods of other people, then what about a Christian Mason or a Christian Odd Fellow who is joined up with those who do not believe in Christ as Saviour, with many who do not believe that the Bible is true, and with some even, as Jews, who do not believe in the deity of Christ, or even with Mohammedans and Hindus? How can the child of God thus yoke up with unbelievers without sin?

In the days of Nehemiah, a terrible sin on the part of God's people was revealed to Nehemiah. Nehemiah 13:23-27 says:

"In those days also saw I Jews that had married wives of Ashdod, of Ammon, and of Moab: And their children spake half in the speech of Ashdod, and could not speak in the Jews' language, but according to the language of each people. And I contended with them, and cursed them, and smote certain of them, and plucked off their hair, and made them swear by God, saying, Ye shall not give your daughters unto their sons, nor take their daughters unto your sons, or for yourselves. Did not Solomon king of Israel sin by these things? yet among many nations was there no king like him, who was beloved of his God, and God made him king over all Israel: nevertheless even him did outlandish women cause to sin. Shall we then hearken unto you to do all this great evil, to transgress against our God in marrying strange wives?"

If it is a sin for a Christian to marry an unbeliever, as it certainly is, then surely it is a sin for a Christian to join in lodges and bind himself into a pact, a "fellowship," an "agreement," a "communion," a "part" with unbelievers so that he cannot reveal the lodge secrets even to his wife!

In Psalm 1:1 the Scripture says:

"Blessed is the man that walketh not in the counsel of the ungodly, nor standeth in the way of sinners, nor sitteth in the seat of the scornful."

That blessing does not belong to any Christian who joins lodges. For every child of God who is a member of a secret order walks in the counsel of the ungodly, he stands in the way of sinners, and he sits in the seat of the scornful.

Lot moved into Sodom, though it was wicked exceedingly before the Lord. The wicked, licentious, and perverted Sodomites became to Lot his "brethren." There Lot grieved his righteous soul with their unlawful deeds. There Lot lost his testimony until he was "as one that mocked unto his sons in law" (Gen. 19:14). There Lot lost his wife; she was turned to salt. There his married children and his grandchildren were burned up in the fire and brimstone from Heaven in God's wrath. And Lot went out of Sodom a ruined man. He took his wine jugs and his two daughters together, finally, to a cave in the mountains; and there, drunk, he ruined the only children he had left alive with the sin of incest. Lot's sin was simply that he yoked up with unbelievers, lived among unbelievers, walked in their counsel, called them brethren. Oh, the heartache and trouble that comes when Christians so sin!

Samson's sin was bad company, also. He ran with the Philistines; he laid his head in the lap of Delilah. He made her his confidante. He told her his secret. How like a Christian joining in with unconverted lodge members and discussing holy things and taking oaths together when he should be with the people of God! And Samson had his eyes put out and was made to turn the mill like a donkey, and then died in his disgrace.

Peter's sin was in stopping to warm by the Devil's fire and in sitting as a friend and brother around the campfire with the soldiers and servants of the high priest who had arrested Jesus and would scourge Him and crucify Him. Peter got in with the wrong crowd and warmed by the wrong fire and entered into the wrong conversation. And before he knew it, his courage was gone. He had compromised his testimony. He lied and swore and cursed and said, "I know not the Man!" And every child of God who yokes himself in bloody oaths with a bunch of unbelievers, who puts himself in their fellowship, is influenced by their opinions, swears to be partial to them above Christians who are not lodge members, and is thus guilty of the sin of Peter. He denies his Lord; he commits blasphemy; he compromises his testimony. When a Christian goes into a place where prayer must not be offered in the name of Christ, where the unregenerate is counted a brother just the same as the born-again Christian, and where, when Scriptures are quoted the name of Christ is omitted and the Scripture is mutilated, then that Christian is guilty of sin. And that is what happens with children of God in the lodge chamber.

I beg you to read again II Corinthians 6: 14-18. Note that God commands us not to be yoked up with unbelievers. You who are saved with the righteousness of Christ should not have "fellowship" with unrighteousness. You who are the light of the world should not have "communion" with darkness. You who are of Christ should not have "concord" or agreement with those that are of Belial. You who believe should not count yourself the same as those who are unbelievers and infidels. You who are saved people are the temple of the living God. God dwells in you. And what agreement should the temple of God have with idols? What agreement have you with those who do not pray in Christ's name, those who are not born again, those who do not love the Lord Jesus? How do you feel at home with the blaspheming, the taking of God's name in vain which is the ordinary procedure in the lodge ritual? With that in mind, I beg you to heed the plain command of God and "come out from among them, and be ye separate, saith the Lord, and touch not the unclean thing" (**II Cor. 6:17**).

CHAPTER IV

It Is a Sin for Christians to Take the Blasphemous and Horrible Oaths of the Lodges

As I took the Entered Apprentice work in the Masonic lodge in 1921 at Decatur, Texas, I took the oath which I am going to give you here. I will give it because I am thoroughly convinced that it was a sin to take the oath; and as a Christian, I ought to renounce it. I feel free to make it known. Particularly, I feel that the oath is not binding upon me because it was required of me under pretenses. The material which it was claimed was secret I have found had been published long ago and is available to every man who wants it and is able to buy it, for fifty cents. Then, it was solemnly promised me that nothing in the oath nor in Masonry would be against my duty to God, to my country, or to my family; and that promise was not true. No court in the land would hold such an oath binding. My conscience does not hold it binding. I have confessed to God my sin and have been forgiven, and I here and now publicly renounce that oath. But here it is—

"I, John R. Rice, of my own free will and accord, in the presence of Almighty God and this Worshipful Lodge, erected to Him and dedicated to the Holy Saint John, do hereby and hereon most solemnly and sincerely promise and swear:

"1. That I will always hail, ever conceal and never reveal any of the secret arts, parts or points of the hidden mysteries of ancient Freemasonry, which have been heretofore, may at this time or shall at any future period be communicated to me as such, to any person or persons whomsoever, except it be to a true and lawful brother Mason, or within a regularly constituted lodge of Masons; and neither unto him nor them until by strict trial, due examination or legal information, I shall have found him or them as lawfully entitled to the same as I am myself.

"2. I furthermore solemnly promise and swear that I will not write, print, paint, stamp, stain, cut, carve, mark or engrave them, or cause the same to be done, upon anything movable or immovable capable of receiving the least impression of a word, syllable, letter or character, whereby the same may become legible or intelligible to myself or to any person under the whole canopy of heaven, and the secrets of Freemasonry be thereby unlawfully obtained through my unworthiness.

"3. To all of this I most solemnly and sincerely promise and swear, with a firm and steadfast resolution to keep and perform the same, without any equivocation, mental reservation, or secret evasion of mind whatever.

"BINDING MYSELF UNDER NO LESS A PENALTY THAN THAT OF HAVING MY THROAT CUT ACROSS, MY TONGUE TORN OUT BY ITS ROOTS, AND BURIED IN THE ROUGH SANDS OF THE SEA AT LOW-WATER MARK, WHERE THE TIDE EBBS AND FLOWS TWICE IN TWENTY-FOUR HOURS, should I ever knowingly or willingly violate this my solemn oath and obligation as an Entered Apprentice Mason. So help me God, and keep me steadfast in the due performance of the same."

Read the above oath most carefully. I will refer to various parts of it again.

Every succeeding degree of Masonry has a bloodthirsty and horrible oath and penalty connected with it as the obligation of the degree.

The above oath is the one I took, and I vouch for it as being true and correct. It was repeated to me many, many times by my father outside the lodge room after it was given to me in the lodge. I took it, a line at a time, not knowing what it was ahead of time, but diligently set out to learn it.

The other oaths of Masonry I did not take, but they are in print through so many sources that an intelligent student can verify for himself their accuracy. The books that give the other degrees give the Entered Apprentice degree just as I took it. If they are right about the Entered Apprentice degree, no doubt they quote accurately the other degrees.

In 1825, the famous Richard Carlisle of England published articles revealing the so-called secrets of Masonry in *The Republican* and afterward in book form, in *Manual of Free Masonry*. In 1826, Captain William Morgan of the Batavia Lodge, New York, wrote out the so-called secrets and mysteries of Freemasonry up to and including the Royal Arch degree. Masons kidnapped Captain Morgan, kept him in old Fort Niagara, and then on the night of the nineteenth of September, 1826, they drowned him in Niagara River. In July, 1828, in LeRoy, New York, a convention of seceding Masons was held with 103 members present, including men who had taken from one to twenty degrees of Masonry. They revealed and exposed the supposed secrets and pretended mysteries of Masonry up to the degree of the Knight of Kadosh. They appointed fifteen Masons of their number, with a preacher, the Rev. David Bernard, as chairman, to write out in proper form all the degrees of Masonry and every rite practiced in this country at that time. That great book was published by the Rev. Mr. Bernard under the title, *Light on Masonry*, and was distributed by the United Brethren Publishing House, Dayton, Ohio and by Ezra A. Cook and Company, Chicago. Besides, the secrets of Freemasonry were written and published by Dr. Robert Morris, Past Grand Master of Kentucky; by President Charles G. Finney of Oberlin College, who had been a Mason; by Rev. J. G. Stearns, who had been a Mason. Edmond Ronayne, Past Master of Keystone Lodge Number 639 in Chicago, wrote out a *Handbook of Freemasonry* and *Masonic Oaths, Null and Void* and other literature, exposing the so-called Masonic mysteries. He gives the oaths in detail. And from him I give some of this material.

Besides, I have before me a Masonic Monitor of 197 pages, most of it in a code which is easily read by one who has been a Mason or taken even one degree. It is published for Masons and used by them in memory work. Thus it will be seen that these oaths are reliably reported, attested to by thousands of men who took them and memorized them.

The Penalties of Masonic Oaths Are Unchristian, Bloodthirsty and Murderous

Read again the penalty assumed by every man who takes the Entered Apprentice obligation:

"Binding myself under no less a penalty than that of having my throat cut across, my tongue torn out by its roots, and buried in the rough sands of the sea at low-water mark, where the tide ebbs and flows twice in twenty-four hours, should I ever knowingly or willingly violate this my solemn oath and obligation as an Entered Apprentice Mason. So help me God, and keep me steadfast in the due performance of the same."

The second degree or Fellow-Craft obligation has the following penalty:

"Binding myself under no less a penalty than that of having my left breast torn open, my heart plucked out, and given as a prey to the wild beasts of the field and the fowls of the air. . . ."

The third or Master Mason's obligation has this penalty:

"Binding myself under no less a penalty than that of having my body severed in twain, my bowels taken from thence and burned to ashes, the ashes scattered to the four winds of heaven, so that no more trace or remembrance may be had of so vile and perjured a wretch as I, should

I ever knowingly or willingly violate this my solemn obligation as a Master Mason. So help me God, and keep me steadfast in the due performance of the same.

And remember that such penalties are connected with the oath required in taking the obligation for each degree.

Such penalties are unchristian. No Christian has a right to bind himself to any such wicked thing.

Every Christian's body is the temple of the Holy Spirit, the dwelling place of God. It is a terrible sin for a Christian to defile his body, and suicide is a form of murder. How, then, can any Christian bind himself to "have my throat cut across, my tongue torn out by its roots, and buried in the rough sands of the sea," or to have his heart plucked out and fed to beasts of prey or to have his body cut in two and his bowels burned? Does any Christian have a right to bind himself to any such penalties? Should any Christian, calling on Almighty God to bear him witness, offer himself and bind himself for any such penalties on the body which is purchased by the blood of Christ on the cross, and which is indwelt by the Holy Spirit, and do all that lest he should reveal some of the silly frumperies and rigmarole of the so-called secrets of Masonry which are widely published and available for scholars all over the world?

But if it is wicked and unchristian for a man to bind himself and offer his body for this murderous mutilation, then is it right for the lodge to administer the oath and assess the penalty, calling upon Almighty God to see it fulfilled? What group of men has the right to murder for the protection of their secret rituals? And every oath with such a penalty assumes that the lodge has a right to execute the penalty and the duty to do it. Oaths vary in various degrees of the Masonic order. In one degree, the drama is enacted of a man seen peeping who is discovered and seized and conducted to death as an example of what is to happen to one so indiscreet as to divulge his obligations. The explanation says, "We are bound to cause their death, and take vengeance on the treason by the destruction of the traitors." The penalty of the obligation for the old Thrice Illustrious Order of the Cross was as follows:

"To all and every part thereof we then bind you, and by ancient usage you bind yourself, under the no less infamous penalty than dying the death of a traitor, by having a spear, or other sharp instrument, like our Divine Master, thrust into your left side, bearing testimony, even in death, to the power and justice of the mark of the Holy Cross." (See *Light on Masonry,* eighth edition, page 199, or Charles G. Finney on *Freemasonry.*)

Certainly Masonic oaths, if taken at their face value, mean that Masonry assumes the right to have assassinated those whom they may count traitors to the order.

But did Masons ever carry out this death threat, this penalty to which every Mason binds himself by oath? The answer is that Captain William Morgan was so murdered by Masons on September 19, 1826. In the book, *Stearns on Masonry*, Elder Stearns, a Baptist preacher, tells how one of the three men who drew lots to take part in the assassination of Morgan, made his confession. It was in 1848, twenty-two years after the Masonic murder of Morgan that the physician, Dr. John L. Emery of Racine County, Wisconsin, took down the deathbed confession of Henry L. Valance, one of the three. After the death of Valance, the confession was made public by Dr. Emery. The confession is found on page 311 of Stearns' book on Masonry and is copied also by the Rev. Charles G. Finney, famous evangelist, in his book on *The Character, Claims and Practical Workings of Freemasonry*, page 11 ff. Some Masons say that Morgan was never murdered. But Masons themselves generally thought so. There were only a few more than 50,000 Masons in the country at that time, and about 45,000 of them quit Masonic lodges, and nearly 2,000 separate lodges disbanded as a result of the great uproar that followed! These figures are given by Evangelist Finney in his book on *Freemasonry*, page 18. The Masonic Grand Lodge at the time defended the murder of Morgan. Many Masons today do so. I discussed the matter with my father freely the summer I started out to become a Mason and have sometimes discussed it since.

The general public also believed that Morgan was murdered, as one of his murderers on his deathbed confessed was true. The Legislature of Rhode Island appointed a committee, gave them authority to arrest and examine Freemasons to see whether the oaths published by Elder Stearns and other Christian men at the time were really the oaths of Freemasons. The committee had before them Masons who had taken the first ten degrees of Masonry, and under the pains and penalties of perjury they owned to the committee that the oaths were those that they had taken. "In 1829, on the trial of Elihu Mather, in Orleans County, the obligations of the three first degrees and of a Royal Arch Mason, were proved, at a Circuit Court held by Judge Gardiner, by the testimony of three seceding Masons and one adhering Mason. In obedience to a resolution of the Senate of New York, Judge Gardiner reported this evidence, and it was printed by order of the Senate." (*Freemasonry*, by Finney; pages 41, 42. May be bought from National Christian Association, Chicago, Illinois.) Fourteen hundred citizens of the state of Connecticut presented a petition to the Legislature in their session of May, 1833, asking that such Masonic oaths be prohibited by law. The House of Representatives appointed a committee to investigate to find whether or not Masonic oaths were given as had been printed by Mr. Allyn in his Masonic Ritual, and by others, and found from witnesses that they were correctly reported with occasional slight verbal differences in various parts of the country. The committee recommended to the Legislature that the oaths should be prohibited by legal enactment:

"1. Because they are unauthorized by law.

"2. They bind the person to whom they are administered to disregard and violate the law.

"3. Because they are, in their natural tendency, subversive of public morals and blasphemous.

"4. Because the penalties attached to the breach of them are such as are entirely unknown to our law, and are forbidden both by the Constitution of the United States and by the Constitution of this State" (*Freemasonry*, Finney, pages 49, 50).

The above evidence shows that the oaths as published were true oaths, and that the general public believed they were sometimes enforced.

It is proper to believe, then, that Masonic oaths are murderous and criminal in intent, and if they are carried out would make every Mason a criminal, a law violator.

It is true that Masons who secede from the lodges are persecuted, slandered and opposed. A few weeks ago a member of a secret order who is also a church member told me how his companions had threatened to beat me up because they disliked what I said in public on this question. There are many known cases where the Ku Klux Klan resorted to violence and some proven cases of assassination. While the Ku Klux Klan is now in general disrepute, it is only fair to remember that members of other secret societies took a leading part in the work of the Klan. That was the case of my father who was both a Mason and Odd Fellow and joined the Ku Klux Klan, also. My father told me of cases of violence by lodge action, which he justified. The spirit of vengeance is inseparably connected with the horrible oaths and penalties of the secret orders.

Lodge Oaths Tend to Protect Criminals, Defeat Justice and Make Lodge Members Into Liars and Deceivers

Again I remind the reader that we are discussing the lodges and not lodge *members*. We are discussing the institutions and not primarily the men and women who are in them. For example, the Master Mason swears, "I will obey all regular signs, summons, or tokens, given, handed, sent, or thrown to me from the hand of a brother Master Mason." And again, "A Master Mason's secrets, given to me in charge as such, and I knowing them to be such, shall remain as secure and inviolable in my breast as in his own, when communicated to me, murder and treason excepted, and they left to my own election." (See *Freemasonry* by Finney, page 44.)

Now, suppose a man is a witness in a criminal case for anything, excepting murder and treason, against a brother Master Mason. Suppose the witness receives a sign, summons or token from the hand of this brother Master Mason who is charged with a crime. He is sworn to retain secrets given to him by his brother Mason in every case, "murder and treason excepted, and they left to my own election." That is, he may feel obligated to hide either murder or treason, but he is not bound to do so, though he is bound to hide any other secret of a Master Mason. Now, in a court of law, can Masons be thoroughly relied upon to witness against Masons having sworn such an oath? Obviously, if they were sincere when they took the oath and regard it as binding, they cannot. And if the lodge oath was taken lightly, may not the oath in court be insincerely taken and lightly held also? This indicates that the oaths of Masonry conflict with the duties of citizenship.

The Royal Arch Mason's oath says, "I will aid and assist a companion Royal Arch Mason when engaged in any difficulty; and espouse his cause so far as to extricate him from the same, if in my power, whether he be right or wrong." Note that last statement of the oath, *"whether he be right or wrong."* He also swears, "A companion Royal Arch Mason's secrets, given me in charge as such, and I knowing them to be such, shall remain as secure and inviolable in my breast as in his own, without exception." Note that this oath does not except either murder or treason as secrets that may be revealed. In some areas the oath has sometimes been given, "murder and treason not excepted." In any case, it is clear that an advanced Mason, taking the seventh or Royal Arch Mason's Degree, swears to keep the secrets of a companion Royal Arch Mason even to the extent of protecting him when guilty of murder or treason, that is, *without exception.* He is sworn to "aid and assist a companion Royal Arch Mason when engaged in *any* difficulty; and espouse his cause, so far as to extricate him from the same, if in my power, *whether he be right or wrong."*

Now, is a Royal Arch Mason on the judge's bench to extricate from his difficulty a Royal Arch Mason brought before him? Is a Royal Arch Mason, then, to be relied upon for jury duty when a companion Royal

Arch Mason is being tried? Can any officer of the law be expected to do his exact duty for the government and justice when another Mason is involved? Obviously, if Masonic oaths mean anything, then a Mason, holding to those oaths and trying to fulfill them as he has sworn to do, would pervert justice and dishonor his office. Otherwise, the solemn and binding oaths are perjury and blasphemy.

Dr. R. A. Torrey, who was superintendent of Moody Bible Institute of Chicago, later dean of the Bible Institute of Los Angeles, world-wide evangelist and Bible teacher, said, "To my own personal knowledge, Masonry has been used to protect criminals and other evildoers from the just consequences of their wrongdoing. In one city where I lived, the proprietor of the vilest and most notorious place in the city could not be touched by the law because he was a Knight Templar. Every other place of the sort was run out of the city but this. I have known similar things elsewhere that have come under my personal observation." (From tract, *My Reasons for Not Joining the Masonic Fraternity,* by Rev. R. A. Torrey, D.D. Printed by National Christian Association)

The oaths of lodge members which bind them to help other lodge members in almost any circumstance, and in some cases without exception, present a great political danger to the nation. Very few men ever run for high office in this country without being lodge members and prominently wearing lodge pins or rings. For this reason, General U. S. Grant, later President Grant, said, "All secret, oath-bound, political parties are dangerous to any nation." John Quincy Adams, Daniel Webster, and other statesmen have recognized this very real danger and openly and publicly opposed secret orders because of it. Certainly Christians should have no part in oath-bound secret orders, binding them with unbelievers by pledges that endanger justice and help criminals.

Lodge Oaths Are Profane and Blasphemous

If a Christian who joins the Masonic lodge, for example, takes the Entered Apprentice oath printed above, "binding myself under no less a penalty than that of having my throat cut across, my tongue torn out by its roots; and buried in the rough sands of the sea at low-water mark, where the tide ebbs and flows twice in twenty-four hours, should I ever knowingly or willingly violate this my solemn oath and obligation as an Entered Apprentice Mason. So help me God, and keep me steadfast in the due performance of the same"—if he is sincere and earnest, then he is entering into an illegal and criminal bond, to be guilty of murder himself or to endorse it in others. But if he is not agreeing to murder in his heart, he is certainly an awful blasphemer.

Notice again the words of the oath. Paragraph three says: "To all of this I most solemnly and sincerely promise and swear, with a firm and steadfast resolution to keep and perform the same, without any equivocation, mental reservation, or secret evasion of mind whatever." If the maker of that oath does not have a firm and steadfast resolution to keep it, then he lies before God and man because he calls on both God and man to witness it. If he has any equivocation or mental reservation, or any secret evasion of mind whatever, about this oath, then he is a falsifier. And remember that all of this is promised and sworn on oath. The obligation is called, "This my solemn oath," and the candidate avows, "I most solemnly and sincerely promise and swear." And the oath closes with this: "So help me God, and keep me steadfast in the due performance of the same." The oath is bloody; it is criminal; it is unchristian; and now certainly it cannot be denied that it is a horrible blasphemy before God!

Consider that God's Word says, "Thou shalt not take the name of the Lord thy God in vain; for the Lord will not hold him guiltless that taketh his name in vain" (Exod. 20:7; Deut. 5:11). Surely anyone who thus calls upon God, most solemnly promising and swearing with a penalty of his own death to keep certain things, and then if he does not with all his heart mean what he says, is he not a profane blasphemer and swearer? Could such a man be believed if he took a simple oath before a court? Could he be trusted on his unsupported promise anywhere?

Reader, look about you and know that every man who is a Mason took these horrible oaths, at least some of them, depending upon how many degrees he has taken. If he was honorable and sincere in his oath, then he is committed to endorse the murder of any who violate that oath and reveal the secrets of Masonry; and on the other hand, if he did not sincerely and earnestly take these solemn obligations on an oath before God, then he is a false swearer, a liar and perjurer, unworthy to be believed and certainly not to be trusted.

Christians, surely you must see that for a child of God to take such unholy, profane oaths is a wicked sin and dishonors Christ.

But blasphemy is the customary thing in the lodges. The name of God is bandied from lip to lip by those who do not love Him and by those who have rejected His Son, Jesus Christ. His name is used as a mere form, without any heartfelt allegiance. For example, the Masonic cry of distress is, "O Lord, my God, is there no help for the widow's son?" The Master of the lodge assumes certain titles that are only fit for Deity Himself, and sometimes actually plays the part of God

Almighty! Usually the name of Jesus is omitted, but in some degrees the name of Jesus and of Christ and other terms like "the Lion of the tribe of Judah" are used again and again. To mention the name of God or of Christ without either sincerely honoring Him or without earnestly calling upon Him in reverent prayer is taking the name of God in vain. And that sin is the sin of every church member who enters into secret orders where the name of God is used as a matter of form and often by unconverted and profane men.

Either lodge oaths mean what they say or they do not. If they do mean what they say, then lodge members are men sworn to crime, to bloodshed, to persecution and even horrible mutilation of the dead. If lodge members mean the oaths they take, then how horribly unchristian they are! How contrary to the law of God and man! How dangerous to good government, how opposed to good morals, how contrary to the commands of Christ! But if, on the other hand, lodge oaths do not mean what they say, and if those who swear so solemnly, calling upon God Himself to witness and keep them steadfast, swearing that they have no mental reservation whatever, no secret evasion of mind—if they do not mean what they swear, then every such lodge member is an awful perjurer, a falsifier, a blasphemer. His promise is a lie, and his oath is perjury! So in whatever sense one may take lodge oaths, they are wicked. To take one is a sin, and nothing but sin can be made of it. Lodge oaths are so wicked that no Christian should ever take one. To do so makes one either a criminal, swearing to break the law and promising to protect others who break it, or it makes one a blasphemer and perjurer!

JESUS COMMANDED CHRISTIANS: "SWEAR NOT AT ALL"

But leaving off the question of whether lodge oaths are bloodthirsty, whether they bind a man's soul and enslave him, whether these oaths pledge a man to murder or violate the law, has a Christian any right to take any lodge oath whatever? The answer comes as clear as daylight from the Lord Jesus Christ Himself, that no child of God has any right to take any such oaths whatever.

In Matthew 5:33-37, Jesus said:

"Again, ye have heard that it hath been said by them of old time, Thou shalt not forswear thyself, but shalt perform unto the Lord thine oaths: But I say unto you, Swear not at all; neither by heaven; for it is God's throne: Nor by the earth; for it is his footstool: neither by Jerusalem; for it is the city of the great King. Neither shalt thou swear by thy head, because thou canst not make one hair white or black. But let your communication be, Yea, yea; Nay, nay: for whatsoever is more than these cometh of evil."

Hear the words of the Son of God: "But I say unto you, *Swear not at all"!* Some Christians believe it wrong to take oaths in court, a judicial oath for government purposes. And because of that the Constitution provides that men may say, "I do solemnly affirm," instead of saying, "I do solemnly swear." Thus the Constitution of our country admits that a Christian is bound in conscience not to take the oaths which are forbidden by Jesus Christ. But the oath in court is simply a solemn assertion that one will tell the truth. If even that legal oath is offensive to some Christians, how can any child of God take the unnecessary, unchristian oath of the secret societies and lodges? Jesus said, "Swear not at all." And He said, "Let your communications be, Yea, yea; Nay, nay: for whatsoever is more than these cometh of evil." A child of God has a right to say, "Yes, yes," and "No, no," and he is expected to be believed. And any Christian who ever goes further than that sins against God. Certainly every Christian who ever took a lodge oath violated the command of Jesus Christ and sinned.

Again in James 5:12 the command is so plain that it cannot be misunderstood:

> "But above all things, my brethren, swear not, neither by heaven, neither by the earth, neither by any other oath: but let your yea be yea; and your nay, nay; lest ye fall into condemnation."

"Above all things . . . swear not," says the Word of God, not by Heaven nor by earth, "neither by any other oath." A Christian is not to swear. And the command says that this is "above all things." What excuse have you, then, Christian man or woman, for taking the ungodly and barbarous oaths of the secret societies? How can you face your Lord and Master whose command is so plain? No Christian, then, can take secret society oaths without sinning against God and violating the command of Jesus Christ and of the Bible.

CHAPTER V

Lodge Religion Is Not the Christian Religion, But Pagan and Antichristian

Many Christian people are in the lodges. They would like to feel that the lodges themselves are Christian and that the lodges make better Christians, or at least that there is nothing offensive to Christianity in the lodges. Unthinking or unspiritual church members often insist that the lodges are just as good as the churches and are doing the same kind of work. Alas, they are deceived. The lodges and secret orders are not Christian. They have a religion, but it is not the Christian religion. The lodge god is not the same as the God of the Bible, the God whom Christians worship through our Lord Jesus Christ. The lodge Bible does not mean the same to a lodge as it means in the house of God and to a devout Christian who believes it. The Lord Jesus Christ is dishonored and unclaimed in the lodges. The doctrine and teaching are antichristian, and doubtless millions of people have died unconverted and doomed to torment, being led by blind leaders of the blind in the lodges. In the lodges they were taught a plan of salvation that cannot save a soul, a plan entirely contrary to the Bible, a plan that is pagan and heathen and not Christian. I say that the religion of the lodges is not Christianity, but that the lodges, in religion, are antichristian.

Again let me say that I do not mean that lodge *members* are necessarily unchristian or antichristian. Many lodge members whom I know give evidence of having truly been born again. I love them and respect them. Many others are as sincere as was my own father, who was a "bright" Mason, an active and enthusiastic lodge member. He was also an Odd Fellow and an ardent Klansman. Whatever his mistakes in this matter, he was an earnest Christian, a godly man who had and deserved the profound respect of Christian people. Many preachers who are saved men, sincere men, are lodge members. They sin in that matter, no doubt, but they are nevertheless Christians. I was a Christian when I came to be made a Mason. So I do not say that men and women who join the lodges are unchristian or antichristian. I am not talking about the lodge *members;* I am talking about the lodges themselves.

No one can deny that the lodges claim to be religious. They do not claim to be definitely Christian, mind you, but they claim to be religious. They talk about God. They have public prayer. The Masonic meeting place is called a *temple*. Lodges have chaplains, priests, Worshipful Masters. They talk about immortality and resurrection and Heaven. Many times the lodges profess to show how to get to Heaven. Bibles are part of the "furniture" of lodges, and frequently Scriptures are quoted. So all will admit that the lodges are religious. Masonry has a religion, but the religion of Masonry is not Christianity. Odd-Fellowship has a religion, though that religion is not Christianity. As far as I know, other secret orders are like these two mentioned. That seems a hard thing to say, that lodge religion is not Christianity but is rather anti-christian and pagan. However, we will prove that that is true, prove it by the lodges themselves as well as by the Bible.

In the *Encyclopedia of Freemasonry* in the Scottish Rite Cathedral in Dallas, I studied at length the Masonic teaching about whether or not Masonry is Christian. This Masonic Encyclopedia was prepared by Dr. Albert G. Mackey, famous Masonic authority. He was the Past General High Priest and Secretary General of the Supreme Council, 33rd for the Southern Jurisdiction of the United States, and it is said that he put more than ten years of labor on this work. The book is certainly considered one of the best, if not the best authority on Masonry. I quote here the article on "Religion" from page 619 (the pages may be different in older editions of the work).

> "The religion of Masonry is not sectarian. It admits men of every creed within its hospitable bosom, rejecting none and approving none for his peculiar faith. It is not Judaism, though there is nothing in it to offend a Jew: it is not Christianity, but there is nothing in it repugnant to the faith of a Christian. Its religion is that general one of nature and primitive revelation—handed down to us from some ancient and patriarchal priesthood—in which all men may agree and none may differ."

Note that this Masonic authority says, "The religion of Masonry is not sectarian." And again, "It is not Christianity." *The religion of Masonry is not Christianity.* "It admits men of every creed within its hospitable bosom, rejecting none and approving none for his peculiar faith."

What is the religion of Masonry, then? This Masonic authority says, "Its religion is that general one of nature and primitive revelation—handed down to us from some ancient and patriarchal priesthood—in which all men may agree and none may differ." In other words, the religion of Masonry is not Christianity, not Judaism, but is that general religion of paganism which all heathen people have. And it is expressly stated that Christians may be received, but they are not approved for their peculiar faith!

In this religion of Masonry, "there is nothing in it to offend a Jew." Therefore, Jesus Christ is left out. Masonry does not teach that He is the divine Son of God and that faith in Him is the only way to be saved. Masonry has no cross in it, no salvation by blood, and its religion is not Christianity, Masonic authorities themselves bearing witness.

Dr. Mackey says elsewhere in the *Encyclopedia of Freemasonry* (page 152 of the edition published by Mose and Company of Philadelphia in 1879):

"Hutchinson and Oliver, I am constrained to believe, have fallen into great error in calling the Master Masons' degree a Christian Institution. If Masonry were simply a Christian Institution, the Brahmin, the Moslem and the Buddhist could not conscientiously partake of its illumination, but its *universality* is its *boast;* in its language citizens of every nation may converse; at its altars all religions may kneel, and to its *creed* every faith may subscribe."

That is the religion of Masonry, and it is not the Christian religion. Masonry, says this Masonic authority so greatly revered among Masons, is not "a Christian Institution." Church members who say that it is are mistaken, says this Masonic author. A Hindu with his religion, or the Mohammedan with his, and the Buddhist with his, all feel alike at home in Masonry just as does the Jew who hates and rejects Christ.

You can see at a glance, then, that the god of Masonry is not necessarily the God of the Bible. Any heathen deity, the god worshipped by any savage, would do as well for Masons. And the religion of Masonry is no more Christian that it is Jewish, and no more Jewish than it is Mohammedan or Hindu or Buddhist, according to Masonic authorities themselves! Those familiar with Masonic literature will recognize this teaching which is very prominent.

Odd Fellows may be surprised to know, if they are not familiar with the teachings of their order, that the official position of their lodge is the same. The Odd Fellows' Manual, written by A. B. Grosh, says on page 297, "Judaism, Christianity, Mohammedanism recognize the only living and true God (page 298); followers of different teachers, ye are worshipers of one God who is Father of all, and therefore ye are brethren." This manual (quoted by Geo. L. Hunt in his pamphlet on *Secret Societies*, printed by Loizeaux Brothers), is understood to have been endorsed by the Grand Lodge and so to be the expression of the lodge itself. Odd-Fellowships, then, recognize Judaism and Christianity and Mohammedanism all on the same plane, and recognize leaders of Judaism and Mohammedanism as equal with Christ. The religion of Odd-Fellowship certainly is not Christianity and does not put Christ above the false teaching of heathendom. The lodges are not Christian!

The book, *Heresies Exposed,* compiled by William C. Irvine (with an introduction by Dr. Louis T. Talbot, president of the Bible Institute of Los Angeles and long pastor of the great Church of the Open Door), is a most useful book on modern heresies. It has a chapter on "Freemasonry" by W. Hoste, B.A. Mr. Hoste calls attention to the fact that "Freemasonry, viewed doctrinally, is Theosophy," and to this sad fact, that the god of Masonry "is a composite deity—Jehovah, Baal, and On, or Osiris, rolled into one, under the initials J. B. O."

If this is true, Masonry is literally idol worship. And remember, it is the boast of Masonry that its religion is the primitive religion of heathen people, the religion of any pagan who might have believed in a Supreme Being!

Read very carefully what Mr. Hoste says:

"Freemasonry, viewed doctrinally, is Theosophy. But, someone may interject, Does it not speak of God, Christ, the Bible, etc.? Yes, like Theosophy, it is heavily camouflaged with scriptural expressions, but used in an unscriptural sense. Without doubt, in general its vocables are the same, but the god of Masonry at any rate is altogether other than the God of the Bible. He is a composite deity—Jehovah, Baal and On, or Osiris, rolled into one, under the initials J. B. O. Novitiates are kept in ignorance of this; they hear the descriptive title, 'the Divine Architect,' and imagine that it is the God of the Bible who is meant. Whereas, if Freemasonry be true, the very idol that Jezebel set up in defiance of Jehovah, and On—one of those gods of Egypt, against which Jehovah 'executed judgment'—share the Godhead with Him. Was it for nothing He gave the commandment, 'Thou shalt have none other gods beside Me' (Exod. 20:3); and said, 'My glory will I not give to another, neither My praise to graven images' (Isa. 42:8)? 'Christ,' too, is on the lips of the Mason, but only in a list of heathen and mythical heroes—Buddha, Vishnu, Baldur, Osiris, Adonis, etc.; all on the same plane, and 'but different labels of the same idea.' A niche has always been offered to Christ in 'the world's *pantheon,'* but He claims the Throne; 'Other foundation can no man lay than that is laid which is Jesus Christ'; 'There is none other name under heaven given among men, whereby we must be saved.' Christ 'in all things must have the preeminence' (I Cor. 3:11; Acts 4:12; Col. 1:18)."

The god of Masonry is not the God of Christianity. Masonry is an unchristian religion, the opposite and the enemy of true Bible Christianity.

The Bible of the Lodges May Be the Koran or Any So-Called "Sacred Book" of Heathen Religions

In the article on the *Bible* on page 104 of the *Encyclopedia of Masonry* by Mackey, so largely used by Masons everywhere, we find the usage of the Bible and the attitude toward the Bible, of the secret orders and lodges. I copied from the *Encyclopedia of Masonry* in the Scottish Rite Cathedral in Dallas, a few years ago, this statement:

"The Bible is properly called a greater light of Masonry, for from the center of the lodge it pours forth upon the East, the West, and the South its refulgent rays of Divine truth. The Bible is used among Masons as a symbol of the will of God, however it may be expressed, and therefore, whatever to any people expresses that will, may be used as a substitute for the Bible in the Masonic Lodge. Thus, in a lodge consisting entirely of Jews the Old Testament alone may be placed upon the altar, and Turkish Masons make use of the Koran. Whether it be the Gospels to the Christian, the Pentateuch to the Israelite, the Koran to the Mussulman, the Vedas to the Brahman, it everywhere Masonically conveys the same idea—that of the symbolism of the Divine will revealed to man."

Masons, then, regard the Bible as only one of many sacred books, the one as good as the other, for Masonic purposes. A Mohammedan can be as good a Mason as a preacher. The Hindu religion fits in as well with Masonry as does the Christian religion, so this Masonic Encyclopedia plainly says.

I have personally talked with Masons who have told me they were present in Masonic lodges in foreign countries when the sacred book used as the greater light was not the Bible, but the Koran, the sacred book of the Mohammedans.

The above quotation is very important. Notice that "the Bible is properly called *a* greater light of Masonry." It is only one of the great lights of Masonry. The square and compass rest on top of the Bible in the Masonic lodge. It is held equal to the Bible as far as Masonry is concerned.

In a Masonic lodge the Bible is only a symbol. It had just as well be the Koran, and it often is the Koran wherever there are Turks or others who are Mohammedans. It may be only the Vedas to the Brahman or Hindu. The Vedas are the sacred writings of these heathen people. So the Bible does not mean in the Masonic lodge as furniture what it means to a Christian. It is only "used among Masons as a symbol of the will of God, however it may be expressed." Certainly you can see that the lodge attitude toward the Bible is not the same as the Christian attitude toward the Bible.

You preachers who join the lodges, you church members in the lodges, is the Koran as good as the Bible to you? Is the Bible to you only a symbol? Or is it really the very Word of God, different from all the other books in the world, the very revelation of God Almighty?

But the lodges quote from the Bible and refer to the Bible. Odd Fellows make much of the parable of the good Samaritan. Masons use the Lord's Prayer and the twenty-third Psalm in their burial services often. They quote other Scriptures. But I remind you that Mary Baker Eddy quotes Scripture to prove her ungodly, Christ-denying, so-called "Christian Science." Mormons quote Scripture to endorse their having many wives, and recently I have found that even Spiritualists quote the Bible and announce themselves as ministers and their groups as churches!

Satan himself quoted Scriptures in the temptation of our Saviour (Matt. 4:6). Jesuits and others used the Bible to justify the hellish inquisition and the murder of Christian martyrs. Yes, the lodges profess to use the Bible, but actually the lodge religion does not regard the Bible as the inspired and authoritative Word of God. The Bible is only a symbol in the lodges, only one of the great lights on the altar, and the Koran would do as well, they say, in countries where the Koran is revered.

In a tract, *The Christian and Secret Societies,* the Rev. Wendell P. Loveless, nationally known Bible teacher, ex-chaplain of the Masonic lodge at Wheaton, Illinois, tells of Masonry's use of the Scriptures as follows:

"MASONRY'S USE OF THE SCRIPTURES"

"Let me give you an example. In probably the best known of the secret orders extant today, I refer to Masonry, the name of Christ is deliberately stricken out from the Scripture passages used in the rituals, where the name of Christ occurs in the Bible in those passages. This is also true of most other lodges. In the charge to be read at the opening of one of the degrees the following Scripture passage is given, 'If so be ye have tasted that the Lord is gracious, to whom coming as unto a living stone, disallowed of men, but chosen of God, and precious, ye also as living stones be ye built up a spiritual house, an holy priesthood to offer up sacrifices acceptable to God. Wherefore also it is contained in the Scripture,' etc. This is a quotation of First Peter 2:5, but please notice that the words 'by Jesus Christ' which occur in the Bible are omitted in the lodge ritual. It is not a misprint; this passage is printed in this mutilated form in other rituals and not only that, but we are assured in a note on one of the passages that it is printed in this form purposely, for it says, 'The passages are taken with slight but necessary modification, from the second chapter of the First Epistle of Peter.'

"Is it a 'slight modification' to take out the name of our Lord Jesus Christ from Scripture passages where it occurs? The name of Jesus Christ is deleted. We immediately see the terrible omission when we realize that the name of the Lord Jesus Christ is the only name in which is salvation.

"Another example is found in one of the other degrees, where Second Thessalonians 3:6 is quoted, 'Now we command you, brethren, that ye withdraw yourselves from every brother that walketh disorderly and not after the tradition which he received of us.' The words 'in the name of our Lord Jesus Christ' are omitted in the ritual. It originally reads, 'Now we command you brethren, in the name of our Lord Jesus Christ, that ye withdraw yourselves,' etc. And then the use of Second Thessalonians 3:12, 'Now them that are such we command and exhort that with quietness they work, and eat their own bread.' Here again the words 'by our Lord Jesus Christ' are omitted in the ritual." (From *The Christian and Secret Societies;*   National Christian Association.)

From many sources I am assured that this is Masonry's way of quoting the Bible, but we use the above quotation because Wendell P. Loveless, long so widely known as a minister and Bible teacher, at the head of WMBI radio station in Chicago, was himself a chaplain in a Masonic lodge, having been initiated into seven degrees.

It must be apparent to the honest reader that the lodges do not use the Bible reverently as the very infallible revelation from God which it claims to be. Anybody who can mutilate the Bible, striking out the name of Jesus Christ and calling that a "slight but necessary modification," in the use of Scripture, does not have the Christian view of the Bible. Surely the religion of the lodges is not the Christian religion.

The Spirit of the Lodges Is the Opposite of the Spirit Commanded of Christians

When I went for the first time into a lodge room, I was struck forcibly by, and the Holy Spirit of God in me was grieved at, the attitude and spirit of men therein. I have mentioned elsewhere the levity about holy things, the profane and careless use of God's name, the oaths, and the association with unchristian and wicked men. But here let us mention further evidences that the spirit of the lodges is unchristian, not the spirit commanded in the Bible for Christian people.

First, the secrecy of the lodges is the very opposite of the Great Commission. The lodge says, "Stay! We have wonderful spiritual lessons, lessons that subdue the passions, lessons that inculcate charity and virtue, lessons to fit men for Heaven. But tell them to no one except lodge brothers, those who have paid for the right to hear. Tell not these lessons to your wife. Tell them not to your son. Only persons of certain age and certain qualifications and certain sex may join your lodge, and that only by paying money or having others pay it for him. To these only, if they be in good standing, having paid their dues, you may reveal the wonderful secrets that bless mankind."

How different is the command of the gospel! The command of Jesus is given in Mark 16:15 as follows: "Go ye into all the world, and preach the gospel to every creature." Again He said, "Go ye therefore, and teach all nations" (Matt. 28:19). The last invitation in the Bible says, "The Spirit and the bride say, Come. And let him that heareth say, Come. And let him that is athirst come. And whosoever will, let him take the water of life freely" (Rev. 22:17).

The contrast is great. The lodges say, "Keep the message secret." But Jesus says, "Tell it abroad." The message is not the same message, and the spirit is not the same spirit in the churches and in the lodges.

There are those who would make us believe that John the Baptist, the Apostle John, even Jesus Himself and other disciples, were members of secret orders. Masonic lodges are "dedicated to God and the Holy Saints John," with shocking blasphemy. But the idea that Jesus or His disciples had anything to do with secret orders is wickedly false. Jesus Himself said, "I spake openly to the world; I ever taught in the synagogue, and in the temple, whither the Jews always resort; and IN SECRET HAVE I SAID NOTHING" (John 18:20).

Jesus said *nothing* in secret. He did no secret teaching and had no part in secret rites such as the lodges have. How wonderful it would be if every preacher of the gospel would follow the example of Jesus

Christ in this matter. Secret things, hidden things, secret signs, passwords, grips, secret lessons—these are not for the church and the Christian. The lodges in their secrecy are the very opposite of the spirit Christ commanded in Christian people. The only reflection that was cast upon Joseph of Arimathaea was that his discipleship was "secretly for fear of the Jews." Christians are exhorted by the Saviour not to hide their lighted candles under a bushel, but rather, "Let your light so shine before men, that they may see your good works, and glorify your Father which is in heaven" (Matt. 5:15, 16).

Again, the lodges shut out the poor. Lodge degrees cost money, lots of money. Lodge dues are heavy. During the depression years there was a great decrease in lodge membership in the United States because the lodges require such heavy fees. Therefore, the lodges do not have room for the poor. Many a man has told me that if he could save the money, he hoped to join the Masons. And several lodges will not receive the lame or the blind, people with one arm or one leg. They may become objects of charity!

But how different is the spirit of the gospel, the spirit of Christ. Jesus, illustrating the gospel appeal, tells the story of a Man who sent out His servant to invite people to come to a great supper. When some would not come, the Master said to His servant, "Go out quickly into the streets and lanes of the city, and bring in hither the poor, and the maimed, and the halt, and the blind." Yet there was more room. And the Lord said unto His servant, "Go out into the highways and hedges, and compel them to come in, that my house may be filled" (Luke 14: 21-23). Thousands of missionaries go to the heart of Africa, live in huts with dirt floors among wild beasts, and teach naked savages; or they go into the interior of China, or to crowded India, or to the South Sea Islands. Missionaries go to the lepers and die as lepers that they might give the gospel to those who cannot pay! In every great city, rescue missions are open to find the drunkard and the harlot, the prodigal boy, the ex-convict, the down-and-outer, the dope fiend, and to bring them, if possible, to Jesus Christ. They are given food; they are given the gospel; they are ministered to with tears and love! I go in a few weeks to spend a week in such a great gospel rescue mission. In such a place I felt the call of God to preach. It is a vital part of Christianity that the gospel of the good news that Christ died for sinners is to be carried to every creature.

But alas, that is not the spirit of the lodges. The lodges are for those who can pay. Members are strictly forbidden under oath to reveal the secrets to others. Masons are sworn not to discuss the things of Masonry with a lodge that has not paid dues to the Grand Lodge (a clandestine lodge), or with a clandestine Mason. In the benediction of a *Masonic Burial Service* before me, the prayer is, "May the blessings of Heaven rest upon us and *all regular Masons."* How different that is from the spirit which would take the gospel to *every creature* as commanded by Christ!

Here is another example. My brother, see if this is the spirit of Christ. The tenth section of the Master Mason's obligation is as follows:

"Furthermore, that I will not have illicit carnal intercourse with a Master Mason's wife, mother, sister or daughter, *I knowing them to be such;* nor suffer it to be done by others if in my power to prevent it."

Notice that this clause of the Master Mason's oath does not forbid adultery or fornication in every case. It does not obligate the Mason not to commit adultery with the wives, mothers, sisters or daughters of others not Masons. It does not even prevent a Master Mason from committing adultery or fornication with the wife, mother, sister or daughter of the Entered Apprentice or Fellow-Craft Mason, those who have had only the first and second degrees. Further, this obligation does not prevent the Mason from committing adultery or fornication with the wife, mother, sister or daughter of a Master Mason, *providing he does not know them to be such.* No, it is a very limited obligation, an obligation that protects only those that he knows to be the wife, mother, sister or daughter of Master Masons.

Is there anything in the Bible like that?

Does Christianity anywhere teach that it is a special sin to commit adultery with a certain very special class who have paid for protection, perhaps, while it would not be such a sin to ruin the sister or daughter or wife or mother of one who has not paid in money for protection, nor entered into a covenant with one, that they will only seduce and ruin the wives, mothers, sisters and daughters of outsiders? Again, I say that the spirit and attitude of the lodges are unchristian, absolutely contrary to the spirit and teaching of Christ.

Again, the proud and haughty arrogance of the lodges directly contradicts the humility commanded of Christians. Jesus said in Matthew 23:5-12:

"But all their works they do for to be seen of men: they make broad their phylacteries, and enlarge the borders of their garments, and love the uppermost rooms at feasts, and the chief seats in the synagogues, And greetings in the markets, and to be called of men, Rabbi, Rabbi. But be not ye called Rabbi: for one is your Master, even Christ; and all ye are brethren. And call no man your father upon the earth: for one is your Father, which is in heaven. Neither be ye called masters: for one is your Master, even Christ. But he that is greatest among you shall be your servant. And whosoever shall exalt himself shall be abased; and he that shall humble himself shall be exalted."

Remember that Jesus is speaking of the Pharisees, those self-righteous hypocrites who outwardly appeared righteous to men but inwardly were full of all iniquity, those who did not believe in being born again and would not submit to Christ as Saviour and Lord. They loved the chief seats; they loved special robes and enlarged borders on their garments. They loved to be called Rabbi and Master. They exalted themselves. But Jesus said that Christians should not be so nor do so. Many, many times in the Bible Christians are commanded to be humble, not to seek the honor of men.

But notice the names by which men call themselves in the secret orders. Here are some titles and terms of the secret orders:

"General High Priest of the General Grand Chapter of the United States."

"Past Grand Patriarch."

"Worshipful Master."

"Sublime Master Elect."

"Grand Master Architect."

"Grand Pontiff."

"Grand Inspector Inquisitor Commander."

"Sublime Prince of the Royal Secret."

Do those titles and terms of the secret orders fit in with the plain command of Jesus Christ for Christians?

And consider the trumpery of the lodges: their plumed hats, their scarlet sashes, their tin swords, their white gloves. Consider their expensive jewels. See processions of lodge members, some as proud as gamecocks in their finery, and others embarrassed and self-conscious in ostrich feathers and sashes and play swords! Do they not remind you of the Pharisees who made broad their phylacteries and enlarged the borders of their garments?

Nay, rather, do they not remind you of little boys wearing Indian suits and cowboy suits, with cap pistols and stick horses? Whether they be Ku Klux Klansmen covered with sheets and pillowcases, or boisterous Shriners with fezzes, or some other order in brilliant dress, do you think the haughty display fits in with the Scripture given above by our Saviour, the Lord Jesus Christ? The Spirit of the lodges, I say, is not the spirit of Christianity. The religion of the lodges is not Christianity but a false and pagan and antichristian religion.

Why do men join lodges? Is it to get out the gospel to the whole world? Is it to win souls? Is it to promote missions? Are the motives of the lodges Christian motives?

Careful thought and investigation will show that the principal motive of lodge membership is selfish.

Men join lodges to gain advancement politically. Masons, for example, are sworn to prefer Masons above others in political matters. Political candidates very often go about giving secret grips and signs to obtain support. When a widely known politician dies, note how many lodges he had joined and how high was his position in them as reported in the papers! The man who was known as the most powerful politician in America, probably not excepting even the President in the first two terms of President Franklin D. Roosevelt's administration, did much of his political work through his contact with lodge men. And lodge men want to elect lodge brothers to office so they may obtain favors or protection, or so the order may be exalted. I say the motive is usually selfish.

Men join lodges expecting to get favors in business, and often do. Particularly, they expect to have help in times of financial distress, in old age, or in sickness. And they very generally hope that their widows and orphans will be cared for by their lodge brothers. The motives are selfish. Again and again preachers have excused themselves to me concerning their lodge affiliation, saying that they feared a time would come when they would not have friends, or when their wives and children would not have support if they did not join the lodges.

This self-seeking, how does it compare with the teachings of Jesus Christ? He who said, "Take therefore no thought for the morrow," and again said, "Seek ye first the kingdom of God, and his righteousness; and all these things shall be added unto you" (Matt. 6:33, 34), surely would not claim the religion of the lodges. The lodges are unchristian, and the religion of the lodges is not the Christian religion but a pagan, heathen, and antichristian religion.

Remember, I do not say that lodge members are not Christian. Some of them are, and some certainly are not. I am not talking about individuals now, but about the institutions themselves. The lodges are unchristian, and their religion is certainly not the Christian religion.

CHRIST IS REJECTED AS SAVIOUR BY THE LODGES

Christianity is not simply a worship of God. The Christian religion involves a coming to God *through Jesus Christ.* Christ Himself said, "I am the way, the truth, and the life: no man cometh unto the Father, but by me" (John 14:6). Jesus claimed emphatically, "I and my Father are one" (John 10:30). The Bible says, "There is one God, and one mediator between God and men, the man Christ Jesus" (I Tim. 2:5). The Old Testament prophecy about Jesus was that He should be called "The mighty God, The everlasting Father" (Isa. 9:6). Christianity and the Christian religion involves recognizing that Christ is God. According to the Bible, God created all things through Christ (Heb. 1:2; Col. 1:16, 17). According to the Bible, it is only by the death of Christ that man's sins can be paid for, and only through faith in Him as Saviour that any man can be saved (John 3:16; I Cor. 15:3, 4; John 5:24; John 3:36). Christianity, then, must be centered around Christ as the only begotten Son of God, the only way that we can approach God for salvation, and the only way we can call upon God acceptably in prayer. Christ Himself, as God, is the heart and center of Christianity.

We have seen that to Masonry and to the Odd Fellows lodges, Christianity is on a par with Mohammedanism and Judaism, and Christ is on a par with heathen teachers. Now let us show further that Christ as the only divine Saviour, with a name above every name, is rejected and denied and crucified afresh in the lodges.

George L. Hunt calls attention to this remarkable fact. The Grand Lodge of Odd Fellows for the State of Massachusetts asked the Sovereign Grand Lodge of the World on February 14, 1889, this question, "Is it lawful for a chaplain to commence and finish his prayer in the name of Christ?" This is given in the report, page 336. Presumably some Christian chaplain, accustomed to praying in the name of Christ as we are admonished to do in the Bible, had tried to do that in the lodge and was rebuked. Here is the answer of the Sovereign Grand Lodge of the World to Odd Fellows:

"Our Order only requires a belief in the existence of the Supreme Being as a qualification for membership, and has no affinity with any religious sect or system of faith; hence EVERYTHING SAVORING OF SECTARIANISM IS NOT TO BE TOLERATED. The words 'system or sect' do not have reference merely to the sects within the pale of Christianity, but have a far broader significance and include all the religions of the world. In this sense Christianity is a sect; hence it is inexpedient, and I think *unlawful* to make prominent references to it in lodge work. We have Jews, and may have Mohammedans and others of non-christian sects within our Order, and the rule applies to them equally with members of the Christian faith."

Remember this is in answer to the question, "Is it lawful for a chaplain to commence and finish his prayer in the name of Christ?" in an Odd Fellows lodge. The answer is a definite "*No.*" Praying in the name of Christ would be "savoring of sectarianism," and according to the Sovereign Grand Lodge of the World for Odd Fellows that "is not to be tolerated." To Odd-Fellowship, Christianity is merely a sect, no better than the religion of Jews who believe that Christ is simply the bastard son of a Jewish harlot, no better than Mohammedanism with its false prophet, Mohammed, which denies the deity of Jesus Christ.

According to the above statement, then, the Order of Odd Fellows "has no affinity with any religious sect or system of faith," so it is certainly not Christian. It "only requires a belief in the existence of the Supreme Being as a qualification for membership." So Odd Fellows certainly are not required to be born again. Any heathen who believes in some god could join that lodge and make a good member.

Christian, how do you feel going into a lodge where you may not pray in the name of Christ, where that is expressly forbidden? How do you feel being in a lodge where you must leave Christ outside lest you should offend those who hate Him and do not believe in Him but who are just as good Odd Fellows as you?

And please remember that that is the ruling of the Sovereign Grand Lodge of the World for Odd Fellows. Could anything be plainer?

The I.O.O.F. was founded by Masons and there got its religious conceptions which are not the conceptions of Christianity. In Masonry, too, Christ is dishonored. A few of the degrees, which are said to be taken from the Old Crusader's ritual, mention Christ, the Saviour, etc., and that ritual was not changed to fit with the general conception of Masonry. But in Masonic degrees in general, and in Masonic literature, it is plainly taught that the religion of Masonry is the religion of Unitarianism, that is, a religion without a Saviour, a religion without the blood of Christ, a religion that does not call Jesus Christ, Lord.

Repeatedly, from many, many sources I have heard that in Masonic lodges it was not proper for people to pray in the name of Jesus Christ as Saviour and Lord. For instance, I have before me a statement by Mr. Wendell P. Loveless. Mr. Loveless was ex-chaplain of the Masonic lodge at Wheaton, Illinois. He says:

"I was regularly initiated into seven degrees of the Masonic Order, holding, for a time, the Office of chaplain in the Blue Lodge, and my knowledge of this society is therefore the result of my experience as a member of it. I now hold a regular demit from the order, which indicates that I was in good and regular standing when I seceded from it." (Page 1, *The Christian and Secret Societies,* by Loveless;   National Christian Association)

After showing how he was compelled by the Lord to leave the Masonic lodge and come out from the unbelievers there, Mr. Loveless says (page 14):

"As Chaplain in the Masonic Lodge, I offered the prayers of the lodge and heard many others offered, but never once in the name of the Lord Jesus Christ. His name is excluded. Certainly it must be very plain that a true believer in Jesus Christ can have no fellowship in that kind of organization. Lodge prayers are not offered in the name of Jesus Christ. The lodge promises the unconverted Jew, the Hindu, the Mohammedan, or any Christ-rejecting sinner who believes there is a Supreme Being, that he may come to the lodge and there find nothing to offend. Since unconverted sinners do not love Jesus Christ, since modernists and rationalists deny that He is the very Son of God, atoning for man's sins, and the only way of salvation, and since Mohammedans and Hindus, like other pagans and heathens, reject Christ and do not accept Him as the Saviour, Son of God and very God, then the lodges shut out Jesus Christ that they may not offend those who hate Him and reject Him!"

A famous Southern Baptist preacher wrote me saying that in a Masonic lodge meeting he prayed and was rebuked for offering his petition in the name of Jesus Christ, God's Son, the only Saviour. Because of that rebuke, showing the utterly unchristian and anti-christian character of the lodges, he discontinued attendance on the lodge.

Before me are two Masonic Burial Services, adopted respectively in 1921 and in 1930 by the Grand Lodge of Texas. In them I have just counted ten separate prayers, not counting the Lord's Prayer, in each. And in the ten prayers, the name of Jesus Christ is not mentioned; the prayers are not offered in His name; no mention of salvation by His blood, nor claiming Him as Saviour, nor of being born again by the Holy Spirit through faith in Him, is made. The religion of the lodges is not the religion of the Lord Jesus Christ. The prayers of the lodges are not prayers in His name. The trust of the lodges is not trust in Christ as Saviour. The hope of the lodges is in good works and not in the blood of Jesus Christ.

Dr. James M. Gray, so long at the head of Moody Bible Institute in Chicago, was everywhere respected as a great Christian and a great scholar. Dr. James M. Gray gave an address, "The Open Confession," delivered at the annual meeting of the National Christian Association in Chicago in 1910, showing why Christians should not be members of lodges. Among other things Dr. Gray said:

"THE LODGE CONCEPTION OF CHRIST"

"I have given some attention also to another of the books just named, 'Morals and Dogma,' prepared for the Supreme Council of the 33rd Degree, Scottish Rite. To be told, as we are in this book, that the Christian Mason sees our Lord Jesus Christ foreshadowed in the divinities of heathenism, and that no one has a right to object if others observe in Him only the 'logos' of Plato; to be told that lost humanity cannot be again united to God, except by long trials and many purifications, and that thus only can men be freed from the calamity of sin; to be told that God has given us powers, by which we may escape from sin, and live calmly, and come off conquerors; to have the square and compass placed upon the same plane as the Holy Bible among the Great Lights of the Order and the furniture of the lodge; and to be told that the doctrines of the Bible are often not clothed in the language of strict truth, and that one who follows the perils and occupations of life in the great training of providence, will require neither the church nor ordinances, except for the expression of his religious homage and gratitude; to make Masonry absolutely superior to Christianity in certain of its teachings, as for instance, in political equality; to be told that at its altars, the heathen, the Christian, the Jew, the Moslem, the followers of Zoroaster can unite in prayer as one; to practically charge the Word of God with inconsistency, and God himself with cruelty, because of the attending sacrifice of blood; such teachings seem sacrilegious and blasphemous in the extreme to the earnest, intelligent Christian.

"They seem unworthy of the endorsement of Christian men, since they are derogatory to the Saviour and destructive of the Gospel of His grace. They are moreover contributing to the culminating sin of the present age, which, according to the New Testament, is the deification of humanity in the person of the man of sin, the Antichrist, and the dethroning of Jehovah in the government of the world.

"These are serious charges indeed, but they are not against any individual, or set of individuals, but against an institution, or a system, if you please. Moreover, if some of my Masonic friends should say that is not a fair, intelligent or candid representation of that institution or system, I can only point them in all sincerity to the authorities that I have named."

Read the above passage by this saintly Dr. Gray carefully again. Surely it adds still further weight to the overwhelming evidence that the religion of the lodges is not only unchristian, but it is definitely *antichristian,* that it dishonors Christ so that no child of God ought ever to be a member of the lodges. Lodge membership is a contradiction of Christianity. It is a compromise for Christians. In the lodges, Christians are "yoked up with unbelievers" and ought to get out.

CHAPTER VI

Lodges Damn Millions of Souls With a False Plan of Salvation That Denies the Blood and Rejects Christ

Where Christ as the Son of God, the dying Saviour, is not honored as Lord, and where the blood of Christ is counted useless, it is certainly to be expected that men would teach a false plan of salvation. And that is true of all the lodges of which we have any knowledge.

The lodges believe in a Supreme Being. "In whom do you put your trust?" one is asked; and then is prompted to say, "In God." But to believe there is a God, or to trust in God without acknowledging Christ as Saviour, will never save a soul. Jesus said, "No man cometh unto the Father, but by me." Jesus is the way to God, the only way to God. To all the lodge people the Word of God cries out, "Thou believest that there is one God; thou doest well: the devils also believe, and tremble" (James 2:19). Any demon in Hell, then, could meet the requirements to join a lodge as far as his religion is concerned, for every demon believes that there is one God. But they are not Christian, and the lodges are not Christian either. Some lodge *members* are Christians, but the lodges did not make them Christian. The lodges are definitely unchristian and antichristian.

What is the plan of salvation offered by the lodges? It must not offend the Jew nor the heathen, so it cannot be salvation by the blood of Christ. It must be acceptable to the heathen Mohammedan or Hindu or Buddhist, so it must not be definitely Christian. What is it then? It is a plan of salvation by character, by human works! The lodges teach men that by joining the lodges, by subduing their passions, by doing good unto others, particularly of their own lodge, that by this growth in character and by these good deeds they will earn and deserve happiness and eternal blessedness hereafter.

In the Masonic Burial Services before me, on page 10, is the conclusion of a Masonic prayer as follows:

". . . and in Thy favor, may we be received into Thine everlasting kingdom, to enjoy, in union with the souls of our departed friends, the just reward of a pious and virtuous life. Amen."

Salvation to a Mason is simply *"the just reward of a pious and virtuous life."* That is salvation by character or by good works and is the exact opposite of salvation by the blood of Christ of undeserving sinners. The Bible teaches one kind of salvation, the salvation which is given sinners by the unmerited grace of God, salvation paid for by the death of Christ on the cross, and received by faith in Him. The lodge teaches that people may "be received into Thine everlasting kingdom" as "the just reward of a pious and virtuous life."

On page 13 of the Masonic Burial Service before me (adopted 1921 by the Grand Lodge of Texas), is a paragraph to be used by the Worshipful Master at the burial service, saying:

"Let the present example excite our most serious thoughts, and strengthen our resolutions of amendment. As life is uncertain, and all earthly pursuits are vain, let us no longer postpone the all-important concern of preparing for eternity, but embrace the happy moment, while time and opportunity offer, to provide against the great change, when all the pleasures of this world shall cease to delight, and the reflections of a virtuous and holy life yield the only comfort and consolation. Thus our expectations will not be frustrated, nor we hurried, unprepared, into the presence of an all-wise and powerful Judge, to Whom the secrets of all hearts are known."

This is clearly a passage on how a Mason is to expect to be saved. The passage speaks of "preparing for eternity" and "to provide against the great change." How is one to prepare for eternity? He is to give serious thought "and strengthen our resolutions of amendment." By amendment, of course, the classic language means to do better, that men are to amend their ways and by a good life are to prepare for eternity. Then when death comes, the Worshipful Master is taught to say, "The reflections of a virtuous and holy life yield the only comfort and consolation." What is the hope of a dying Mason? What is his ground for believing he will have everlasting life and happiness in Heaven? Why, his virtuous and holy life is his only comfort and consolation, evidently his only hope for salvation! "Thus our expectations will not be frustrated, nor we hurried, unprepared, into the presence of an all-wise and powerful Judge, to Whom the secrets of all hearts are known."

The Mason, then, is taught to expect that if he will amend his life so that he has a virtuous and holy life, he need not be afraid to face death, but will be prepared when he comes to face the Judge who knows all the secrets of his heart! In other words, Masonry teaches that if people will amend their lives and live virtuous and holy lives, then they will come and be judged on the basis of their works and thus can be saved!

In the following paragraph Masons are urged to "support with propriety the character of our profession, advert to the nature of our solemn ties, and pursue with assiduity the sacred tenets of our Order." And the inference is plainly given, that by thus being good Masons, "we may be enabled to prosecute our journey without dread or apprehension, to that distant country, from whose bourne no traveler returns."

Masonry teaches salvation by character and works, or, in other words, it teaches salvation by being good Masons!

In fact, Masons often say that if one lives up to his Masonic obligations, he will be saved. That is the plain teaching of Masonry itself. For instance, in the Masonic Burial Service, adopted by the Grand Lodge of Texas in 1930, pages 13 and 14, is the following statement in the Master's oration at the grave:

"This apron we deposit in the grave of our brother as a reminder of our unity in service, of the common destiny that beckons us hence, of the Masonic spirit of universality that linked us as brothers, and, although barriers of wealth, political power or social prestige may have kept us temporarily apart, Death, the great leveller, brings us at last to one distinction, reduces us to a common grade, makes us to know that, born as we are into one great brotherhood, no circumstance of chance or achievement shall serve to separate us in Eternity."

The theme is the universality of Masonry and the statement here made is to be made of all Masons who ask for a Masonic burial, whether they be Christian or unchristian, Jew, Moslems, Hindus in religion, whether they believe in Christ or hate Him and reject Him. And notice the plain statement that "Death . . . makes us to know that, born as we are into one great brotherhood, *no circumstance of chance or achievement shall serve to separate us in Eternity."*

Study that sentence again. It says (1) that Masons will never be separated in eternity. That is mentioned in the following paragraph as "blooming in everlasting beauty in the garden of our Father and our God," and then later as "Eternal Spring." All Masons, then, according to this passage, will be united in Heaven. (2) The passage above says that that is achieved because Masons are "born as we are into one great brotherhood." According to the plain meaning of that passage, people are saved by being Masons, go to Heaven by being Masons.

Mackey's *Encyclopedia of Free Masonry* likewise teaches that Masons are saved, not through faith in Christ by His grace, but by their own good deeds. Under "APRON," that Masonic authority says:

"By the lambskin the Mason is reminded of that purity of life and rectitude of conduct which is so essentially necessary to his gaining admission into the Celestial Lodge above, where the Supreme Architect of the Universe forever presides."

Here are other statements of this admitted authority and widely used *Encyclopedia of Free Masonry,* teaching that men are saved, not by the atoning blood of Christ through faith, but by human goodness.

Under "Definitions of Freemasonry": " 'The definitions of Freemasonry,' says Oliver in his *Historical Landmarks of Freemasonry,* 'have been numerous; but they all unite in declaring it to be a system of morality by the practice of which its members may advance their spiritual interest and mount by the theological ladder from the lodge on earth to the lodge in heaven.' "

Under "Master Mason": "As a Master Mason he is taught the last, the most important, and the most necessary of truths, that, having been faithful to all his trusts, he is at last to die and to receive the reward of his fidelity."

I insist that this is the universal teaching of Masonic leaders, and of most other lodges. They do not believe in Christ as the only Saviour, and that is the reason lodges usually do not have prayers in Jesus' name and why His name is cut out of Scriptures quoted in the lodges. Lodges have a false plan of salvation that denies any need for the blood of Christ to save sinners.

Any time, then, that a Christian talks to a Mason and urges him to turn to Christ and be saved, and the Mason answers that he does not need salvation because he is a Mason, that the Masonic lodge is as good as the church, and that if a Mason lives up to his obligations he will get to Heaven all right without Christ; then you may know that this unconverted Mason is saying exactly what he has been taught in the lodge.

Again I repeat it, the lodges are not Christian in their religion. They are antichristian. They teach a false plan of salvation, a plan that never saved a soul, a plan that is of Satan and not of God, a plan that takes honor from Jesus Christ and gives it to the lodges and to the lives of men. Every Christian worker who earnestly tries to win souls finds lodge members who are trusting in their lodges, trusting in their good deeds, and who will not hear the gospel that they need to be born again and must trust in Christ or be forever lost. Every Christian in the lodges is to blame for that awful sin. They have blinded the eyes of the unconverted; they have taught in the lodges or have lent their presence and their influence to the teaching of the lodges that people are saved by just and virtuous lives, or by obeying the maxims and the precepts of the lodge. Every preacher who preaches the gospel of salvation by grace and by the blood of Christ in a church, and then is a member of a lodge, is damning souls in one place while he tries to save them in another.

But I have not twisted the teachings of the lodges. I have not read into their teachings what they do not mean. Intelligent and highly advanced lodge members themselves agree that their teaching is salvation by character instead of salvation by the merits of the shed blood of Jesus Christ.

Before me is a booklet of twenty pages, put out by the American Unitarian Association, 25 Beacon Street, Boston, Massachusetts. The title is, *"The Relation of the Liberal Churches and the Fraternal Orders."* It is written by Elijah Alfred Coil who died in 1918. He was minister of the First Unitarian Society (sometimes called church), Marietta, Ohio, until his death. He was also Master of the Masonic Lodge at Marietta, Ohio. (Though that fact is not printed on this pamphlet, it is printed elsewhere.) In this tract, put out by the Unitarians, is an appeal to the lodge members to turn away from the orthodox churches who hold to the old-time fundamentals of salvation by faith in Christ as Saviour. This lodge man writes the entire tract to his brothers, showing that the only way one can be true to the teaching of the lodges is to leave the orthodox churches that believe in salvation by blood and enter the so-called liberal churches that deny salvation by the blood of Christ and teach salvation by character and good works. The entire booklet is written for that purpose.

And the man is right. If the lodges have the right plan of salvation, then the orthodox, old-time churches that believe and preach salvation by the blood of Christ are wrong. If the lodges are right, then the modernists, the rationalists, the so-called liberal churches are right. By "the fatherhood of God and the brotherhood of man," Unitarians and modernists who deny salvation by the blood of Christ mean that God is the Father of all men without their needing to be born again, and that all men are brothers alike under God, and that there is no such thing as a distinction between people saved by faith in Christ and those condemned because they have not received Christ. In other words, the phrase both to the lodges and to the modernists (or liberals or Unitarians) means the same, and it denies the fact that men are lost, that men must be born again, and that one is a child of God only by being born again. Now read the following passage from pages 10 and 11 of this tract by a Unitarian minister and Master of a Masonic lodge:

"Nearly all of those monitors [monitors of the lodges, he means—J.R.R.] have, as their very heart, the fatherhood of God, the brotherhood of man, immortality, and salvation by character, principles very familiar to every Unitarian Sunday School scholar who has been properly taught the fundamentals of our faith.

"That the fundamental difference in the principles embodied in the historic creeds of Christendom and those of our modern secret orders has not been clearly thought out is indicated by the fact that many pledge themselves to both. There are lodge men who, in the churches, subscribe to the doctrine that 'We are accounted righteous before God only for the merit of our Lord and Saviour, Jesus Christ, by faith and not for our own works or deservings,' and enthusiastically join in the singing of hymns in which that idea is embodied. Then in their lodge meetings they just as enthusiastically assent to the following declaration: 'Although our thoughts, words and actions may be hidden from the eyes of men, yet that All-Seeing Eye whom the sun, moon and stars obey, and under whose watchful care even comets perform their stupendous revolutions, pervades the inmost recesses of the human heart, and will reward us according to our merits.' A little child, once its attention is called to the matter, ought to be able to see that it is impossible to harmonize the creed statement here quoted, with the declaration taken from the monitor of one of our greatest and most effective secret orders, and found, in substance, in the liturgies of nearly all the others. If 'We are accounted righteous before God only for the merit of our Lord and Saviour, Jesus Christ, by faith and not for our own works or deservings,' then it cannot possibly be true that the All-Seeing Eye 'Pervades the inmost recesses of the human heart, and will reward us according to our merits.' One of these declarations excludes the other. Men cannot consistently subscribe to both."

The above, remember, is written by a Unitarian minister who was also a Master Mason. It is the position of the modernist or the unbeliever in Jesus Christ and is likewise the position of the lodges. Very carefully and strikingly it calls attention to two plans of salvation. Real Christians believing the Bible agree that "we are accounted righteous before God only for the merit of our Lord and Saviour, Jesus Christ, by faith and not for our own works or deservings." That is exactly what I believe

and what all born-again Christians must surely believe. It is certainly
what the Bible teaches. But the lodge position and the position of
Unitarians and modernists and all who reject salvation by the blood
and yet believe in a Supreme Being is "that the All-Seeing Eye 'Pervades
the inmost recesses of the human heart, and *will reward us according to
our merits.'* "

In the same paragraph the author continues, quoting Billy Sunday
as saying, "The fatherhood of God and the brotherhood of man are
the worst rot ever dug out of hell," and then bemoans the fact that
lodge men sometimes went to hear Billy Sunday and seemed to approve
his utterances! The argument is that those who believe in salvation
like Billy Sunday preached it, by the blood of Christ, could not possibly
be true to the doctrine taught in the lodges, and that those who believed
in the fatherhood of God without a need of being born of God, as the
lodges do, should not approve Billy Sunday's doctrine of the blood.
The pamphlet continues, urging upon lodge members to take their
children out of orthodox Sunday Schools where they are taught that they
are saved through the merits of Jesus Christ by faith and not of their
own deservings, and to place these children in Unitarian Sunday Schools
where they will be taught salvation by their own character. On page
15 Mr. Coil says:

> "Fraternity men, interested in the welfare of their children,
> should be informed that in the liberal churches [modernist and
> Unitarian churches, he means—J.R.R.], their children will be
> trained in principles which they will not practically have to deny,
> should they become members of the lodge."

Beyond any shadow of a doubt, then, the lodges deny the gospel
of Jesus Christ. They are blind leaders of the blind, leading millions of
men and women away from Christ, away from the Bible, away from
salvation by the blood. They lead them to depend upon their own
righteousness and doubtless lead them to feel no need of regeneration,
lead them to ignore the warnings of the gospel, and so lead them to fall
at last unprepared into a devil's Hell! How many poor sinners who die
depending on the lodges and their good works will rise to confront
the preachers and church members in the churches who were also
members of the lodges!

Stephen Merritt, an undertaker, later a mission superintendent and
Christian editor and soul-winning layman, filled with the Spirit, had an
experience that ought to warn many others. He was Master of the biggest
lodge in New York in the time of the Civil War. He says:

"But I found the tendency of the whole thing evil, and only evil, continually. So I protested and left, but still I paid dues and attended funerals. I was a very dull scholar.

"One incident helped to open my eyes. I have always preached that there is no other name but Christ by which we can be saved. But again and again I found Masons dying without God and without hope. I was called to the bedside of one member of my lodge who was thought to be dying. He gave me the grip as I sat down by him. He said he was dying and was in great distress for his soul. I tried to have him look to Christ. But he reproached me, saying I had led him astray. I had told him in the lodge, as Master, that a moral life was enough. He said, 'You told me then that it was all right if I was an upright man, and obeyed the precepts of the lodge, but I am leaning on a broken reed; and now I am dying without God. I lay this to your charge, Worshipful Master. I leaned on you and now I am dying.'

"I groaned in agony and fell on my knees and cried to God to spare the man's life. My heart was almost broken. God heard, and spared the man, but he has since died a Christian. He was converted, and told me I must get out of the lodge; that I could not be consistent as a Christian and a Mason. But I did not see it. Ministers and other good men are in the lodge. They help to make it a delusion and a snare. The times of such ignorance God winked at, but now every man is commanded to repent of lodge folly."

I beg you, reader, whether you be a man in the lodge, or a woman, or even a boy in the De Molays, to come out from the lodges before you are responsible for the damning of souls! The plan of salvation brought by the lodges is that of Cain who would have no bloody sacrifices but brought the fruit of his toil. The plan of salvation taught by the lodges is like that of the Pharisee who went up into the temple to pray and said, "God, I thank thee, that I am not as other men are, extortioners, unjust, adulterers, or even as this publican" (Luke 18:11). But that Pharisee, for all his self-righteousness, was still a poor, condemned, ruined sinner. He needed to come like the poor publican who stood and prayed, "God be merciful to me a sinner" (Luke 18:13), and went down to his house, Jesus said, "justified rather than the other." Poor Cain needed to learn the secret of Abel, who by faith brought his bloody sacrifice, looking forward to the coming of the Saviour whose blood could pay for man's sins.

Some man will read this, perhaps, who is a member of some lodge but who does not know what it means to really be born again by depending wholly on the shed blood of Jesus Christ. It may be you have been blinded by the trappings and teachings of the lodges. It may be you have depended upon living a good life, on subduing your passions, on doing good to others, and thus you have fallen into the trap that Satan has set in the lodges for souls. I beg you, in Jesus' name, to flee to the Saviour! Admit that you are a sinner, repent of your sins and trust Jesus Christ to forgive and save you. His blood was shed for all of us who were aliens and strangers from God by nature and must be born again if we ever see God in peace. Only those who trust Jesus Christ as a personal Saviour from sin are saved and fit for Heaven.

Again let me say it, that you may never forget it—the salvation offered and taught by the lodges is a false salvation on a plan that is contrary to the Bible, a plan that dishonors God, rejects the blood atonement of Jesus Christ, a false plan that damns every poor soul who trusts in it!

THE DEADLY RESULTS OF LODGES TEACHING SALVATION BY CHARACTER, DENYING BLOOD OF CHRIST

We have shown that the lodges almost unanimously teach the fatherhood of God and the brotherhood of man; that is, salvation by character, salvation by a just and holy life, instead of salvation by the blood of a crucified Saviour. Lodge leaders and teachers and literature and rules being witness, the fraternal orders do not believe and do not teach salvation by faith in the shed blood of Christ, the Lamb of God which taketh away the sin of the world.

This false doctrine pervades all our churches. For years I wondered why it was that even in areas where moderism as such made no headway in the churches, where pastors and teachers still professed to believe in the inspiration of the Bible and the deity and atoning blood of Christ and in salvation by the blood; I wondered why at least half of the people in the churches still believed that salvation depended on human goodness and human works. Why was it? It seemed unexplainable. But when one remembers that every principal lodge in America systematically and subtly teaches under the most solemn surroundings that men are saved by character alone, that there is no need for a new birth since all men are brothers and God is Father of all, that the Mohammedan or the Christ-rejecting Jew is as good as a Christian, then it is easy to understand whence comes this terrible doctrine. "A little leaven leaveneth the whole lump" (I Cor. 5:6). Church members in the lodges are constantly spreading this blood-denying, Christ-rejecting, hellish doctrine until it pervades the thinking of unregenerate men everywhere and subconsciously forms a part of the thinking even of many preachers and of hosts of truly converted church people.

In countless individual cases I have met it. Sinners unconverted, unrepentant, unregenerate, feel no need for Christ and the new birth. They insist continually that if they live up to the obligations of the lodge, or if they live moral and virtuous lives, they will get to Heaven. I charge that this error, which is probably responsible for the eternal damnation of more individuals in America than any other, is directly fostered throughout the nation by the lodges. And I charge that the lodges themselves are the most potent influence to teach people to depend upon their own righteousness and character instead of the blood of Christ. Every evangelist, every soul-winning pastor, every personal worker has met continually with individuals who are blinded to God's plan of salvation because they accepted the lodges' false and satanic plan of salvation which leaves out the blood of Christ.

This doctrine largely neutralizes the preaching of the gospel everywhere. How can the public take seriously gospel preaching, evangelistic preaching, preaching that demands repentance and regeneration, on the part of any preacher who wears the Masonic emblem or who is the chaplain or a member of an Odd Fellows lodge? The preacher himself does not intend it, but the influence of the lodges, which he helps to promote, works continually to blind people to the gospel he preaches. The only preacher who could be perfectly at home with the lodges and be consistent as a preacher and a lodge member is the Unitarian or modernist who does not accept the Bible as God's own divine revelation and Christ as the Lamb of God nor His blood as the only hope of sinners.

The blight of death, as far as soul-winning fire is concerned, comes on the churches where leading members are devoted to the lodges. One fact which led me to preach on this subject and to write this series of articles was that my heart was broken because I could not lead some of the best people in my church to win souls. The men who were best informed, most influential, the men with best business judgment, the men most looked up to in the church, moral, kindly, intelligent, sincere men, I found, never did win souls. The burden of it broke my heart. I pondered on it for months and months. One Sunday night, preaching on the death of Christ on the cross, I mentioned the Pharisees who sat about the cross watching Jesus die, like grinning jackals, waiting the death of the prey. I said that these self-righteous Pharisees, unregenerate, Christ-rejecting, were like church members and lodge members who are moral and upright but do not accept Christ as Saviour. Some lodge men, friendly toward the church, were offended. Discussion arose about it, and I found that nearly all these principal men whose lack of interest in revivals, whose inability or unconcern about soul winning and whose lukewarmness had broken my heart, were lodge members! And everywhere else I have found it so—lodge membership and imbibing lodge teaching spells the death knell to soul winning. It kills the concern of a Christian for dying souls. This awful, Christ-rejecting doctrine that men are saved if they live up to their obligations, that men are saved by pious and good lives—that, I say, is the deadly enemy of evangelism and soul winning.

This doctrine is the deadly enemy also of foreign missions. Missionaries who have nursed at the breast of fraternal orders have been taught that the Koran is as good as the Bible, just so it symbolizes the will of God; that any god is as good as the Christian God, just so he is believed to be a supreme being; have been taught that a Mohammedan is just as sure of Heaven as a Christian if he keeps his lodge obligations and lives a moral life; they have been taught that the Christ-rejecting Jew is just as safe, if he has a good character, as a Christian. How is such a missionary going to appeal to heathen people to reject their religions and turn to Christ alone? Rather, such "missionaries" found schools, teach English, teach social progress, and try to combine the so-called "good features" of Christianity with the "good features" of Buddhism or Hinduism or Mohammedanism! But I solemnly declare unto you that Christ will accept no equals, and the Bible will never admit being placed on the same basis as the Koran and the writings of Buddha. It is not Bible Christianity which does not demand absolute surrender to Christ as Lord of all. The missionary aim and the missionary heart is gone when lodges sell their doctrine that people are saved by moral living, by curbing their passions, by keeping their obligations. There is no salvation in any doctrine except faith in the shed blood of Christ. And the lodges take away that gospel, leaving preachers and missionaries with no saving message.

What Lodges Did to My Father

Let me open my heart and speak as reverently as I know how about my dear father who has been in Heaven now since 1930. My father, as I remembered him in my early childhood, was a devout and most useful minister of the gospel, a pastor of small Baptist churches. Our home was a home for preachers. It was the home of orthodoxy. None of us ever conceived the idea that one could be a Christian without believing the Bible, and we knew nothing of any plan of salvation but by trusting in the shed blood of Jesus Christ. My father's preaching was much in demand. He was blessed in revivals. With only an ordinary education, he had an unusual fervency and a practical, intelligent grasp of the essentials of the Christian faith. When I was born, my father and mother dedicated me to God and prayed that I might be a preacher. When I was five, my mother died, and on her deathbed had us sing—

> "How firm a foundation,
> Ye saints of the Lord,
> Is laid for your faith
> In His excellent Word!"

And then she made us promise to meet her in Heaven. Our home was a godly home. All of us went to services every time the church doors were open. Revivals were dear to the heart of my father. He was a fervent advocate of foreign missions and a most liberal giver.

But before I was grown, my father joined the Odd Fellows lodge. Later he joined the Masonic lodge. His interest in the lodge work grew continually. Though in middle life, he was called a "bright" Mason, and the memory work he was able to do was counted very unusual for a man of his age. He became in demand as a lodge lecturer. Night after night he would drive far across the country to take part in lodge meetings at various places. He was offered a full-time position as a Masonic lecturer. His contacts were many and, I think, his influence was great.

But as his interest in the lodges grew, something happened to his spiritual life. I remember when a Baptist church called for him to fill the pulpit and he refused, excusing himself on the plea, "I am rusty." His mind had not been on the Bible and on preaching the gospel!

His mind was taken up more with business affairs. He ceased preaching altogether. Finally, less and less did he attend the Baptist church where his membership was. At last he went for two full years without once entering the doors of the good church where his membership was, except for funerals.

And his doctrine changed likewise. I remember how startled I, a young preacher, was when he told me he thought Socrates, the ancient Greek philosopher, was just as truly saved as Christians are, though he knew nothing of Christ. He said that he believed sincere heathen people who had a religion and earnestly tried to live up to their light were saved and did not need to be born again. My father first left the ministry. Then he ignored the local church. He said the seats were too hard; yet he would stay until one o'clock in the morning at a lodge meeting! Then his interest in missions and evangelism waned. I grieved about it but did not know it was the natural fruitage of the seed planted by the lodges. He was an apt pupil. He absorbed the lodge teaching. It led him away from the Bible, away from the ministry and soul winning, away from the church.

When I went into the lodge to be initiated into the Entered Apprentice degree, I was horribly shocked to see my father the boon companion of a practical infidel, a blasphemer, a denier of the virgin birth and the atoning blood. I never went back to the lodge.

The years came and went. In the providence of God, in 1929 I went to Decatur, Texas, for a tent revival. My father, with a dad's love and pride in his son, helped me make arrangements for setting the big tent. With his car hooked to the block and tackle, he helped lift in place the big center poles of the tent. And when the opening night came, my father sat in a cane-bottom chair, leaning back against a tent pole. His face was all aglow, and his eyes were misty, not, at first, with the gospel but rather in his pride over his boy and the big tent and the great crowds.

The gospel in that independent revival was the power of God, the dynamite of God! As I preached and wept and prayed over such themes as sin, death, Hell, judgment, the return of Christ, and being born again, hundreds of sinners were saved. There was a mighty moving of the Spirit, and the town was shaken. For a few nights my father sat and took it all in. But he was really a saved man. In his heart he did love God. The Spirit of God dwelt within him. Before long the tears were rolling down his cheeks. I will never forget the night when he left his chair at the invitation time and went back to the back of the big tent and put his arms around an old cursing, sinning neighbor and won him to Christ. After that it was an every night's occurrence. Out of some three or four hundred professions of faith, I suppose he must have won twenty. The joy of salvation came back, his concern about sinners came back. Oh, I have thanked God a thousand times that it was my privilege to go back and preach to my dad and to have fellowship with him in the gospel, to see his faith renewed and his interest in saving souls revived.

In 1930, I was in a revival in Duke, Oklahoma. My father had had a stroke two years before but had rallied. He felt so proud that he could get in his car and drive in to Oklahoma to be in this revival. He was there two days and won four men, heads of families, to Christ. He was greatly beloved by lodge men; so a committee came to see him to prevail upon him to leave the revival and go out to the lodge and speak. But that afternoon my father was stricken at 4:30 and died at 6:30. I know he is with the Lord, and I know that he rejoices with joy unspeakable that his son is trying humbly and earnestly, and sometimes at heavy cost of friends, to preach the gospel, the old gospel, the gospel he preached in his youth and believed again and carried again to others when he returned to the Lord in his old age.

My father never left the lodge. At his funeral this infidel crony had a large part in the ceremony which taught that my father, by a pious and holy life, was assured of the right to enter into Eternal Spring, in the presence of the Great Architect of the universe, where all Masons would be assembled together. But that Masonic funeral slandered my father's belief and denied his testimony. He knew he was saved by the blood of Christ alone, without any merit of his own. I know I speak what he would have me say and what God would have me say when I warn Christians that the lodges put a blight upon soul winning and teach people that they do not need the blood of Christ.

Church members in the lodges, you must give an account to God for an unchristian religion that damns multitudes and bars the way between unregenerate sinners and the only possible true hope of salvation. How can any man stay with an institution that so blinds sinners and damns souls and nullifies the gospel of the grace of God?

CHAPTER VII

Lodges Are a Swindle

Another good reason for Christian people to avoid the lodges is that there is a certain insincerity and dishonesty about the lodges that a child of God ought not to take part in. Lodges, in many respects, are a swindle.

First of all, the claim of the lodges to secrecy is dishonest and untrue. Men pay great sums of money for degrees in the lodges, acting on the claim of the lodges that these degrees have secret "work," wonderful verbal lessons that have never been put in writing, and that would not be available any other way.

But that claim is utterly false. Literally dozens of Masons, from Richard Carlisle on down, have renounced Masonry and then put in print the secret signs and grips and oaths and degrees and symbolism of Masonry. Before me are advertisements from one publisher, giving some fifteen or twenty books by Masons and for Masons, giving the secret work of the lodges. Masons themselves, high up and leading Masons, use these books to refer to and by which to check the memory work. Also the same publisher advertises The Complete Revised Ritual of the Lodge, Encampment and Rebekah (ladies') Degree of Odd-Fellowship. It was written by a Past Grand Patriarch of the lodge. Here advertised also is the revised and amended official "Ritual for Rebekah Lodges, published by the Sovereign Grand Lodge, I.O.O.F." with Unwritten (secret) work added and the official "Ceremonies of Instituting Rebekah Lodges and Installation of Officers of Rebekah Lodges." Here also are advertised other secret society rituals, Knights of Pythias, Modern Woodmen, Red Men, Knights of the Maccabees, and others.

Here in my hand is a Masonic Monitor, *King Solomon and His Followers,* called "a valuable aid to the memory, strictly in accordance with the latest authors," published by the Allen Publishing Company, John and Dutch Streets, New York. This Monitor, used by Masons themselves, is mostly written in a very easy code so that an intelligent man with just a little study can make out practically every word of it.

I say that the claim of the lodges to give secret and wonderful lessons not available in any other way is false, and in this the lodges are a swindle. Not only are the lessons ordinary, but they are not secrets to those who can read and will seek the truth.

Some of the lodges, particularly the Masonic lodge, lay claim to a very great age. Some Masons claim that Masonry is of divine origin. Some say that Noah and Enoch passed on secrets to Masonry, and it is generally claimed that King Solomon himself organized a Masonic lodge. It is said that Zechariah was a Mason. The lodges are "erected to God and dedicated to the Holy Saints John," referring to John the Baptist and John the apostle, both of whom, it is claimed, were patrons of Masonry. In the Masonic Burial Service, adopted by the Grand Lodge of Texas in 1921, is this statement, "This white apron (or lambskin) is the emblem of innocence and the badge of a Mason; more ancient than the golden fleece or Roman eagle; more honorable than star and garter, when worthily worn." Note that this "badge of a Mason" claims to be *"more ancient than the golden fleece or Roman eagle."*

Now all this is a wicked falsehood, a lie concocted to deceive the simple and ignorant. In this matter Masonry is such a hoax, such a dishonest swindle, that Christian men ought to be ashamed to be connected with it. As the great John Quincy Adams said about Masonry:

"If the candidate has been educated to a sincere and heartfelt reverence for religion and the Bible, if he exercises his reason, he *knows* that all the tales of Jachin and Boaz, of Solomon's Temple, of Hiram Abiff, and Jubela, Jubelo and Jubulum, are impostures—poisons poured into the perennial fountain of truth—traditions exactly resembling those reprobated by Jesus Christ, as making the Word of God of none effect" (quoted from *Masonic Oaths Null and Void*, by Edmond Ronayne, page 135).

Edmond Ronayne, who was Past Master of Keystone Lodge Number 639 in Chicago, says about the frauds of Masonry:

"Then it is seriously asserted that Hiram Abiff was slain at *high twelve* near the east gate of the Temple, by one Jubulum, when the real facts are that Hiram was not slain at all, and that the Temple of Solomon had no 'east gate' to it. And in connection with this pretended murder we are also further assured that the three assailants of Hiram—Jubela, Jubelo and Jubulum—

were workmen from Tyre, whose names had three Latin termina-
tions sixteen centuries at least before the Latin language was
ever known.

"Again it is related of Hiram that he was slain at *high twelve*
and concealed in the rubbish of the Temple, while the truth is
that there was no rubbish whatever around the Temple, and he
could not have been murdered and concealed as related, without
the ruffians being at once detected.

"Again, it is asserted of Hiram Abiff, that he cut a white
stone, and polished and engraved upon it eight Roman letters—
H, T, W, S, S, T, K, S—the initials of Hiram, Tyre, Widow's
Son, Sent to King Solomon—at least fifteen hundred years before
the Roman letters were known in the world" (*Masonic Oaths
Null and Void,* pages 138, 139).

All this talk about the ancient origin of Masonry is false. Masons
themselves have kept a careful record of the origins of Masonry. By
consulting a standard encyclopedia, the reader may learn accurately
about the origin of Masonry.

The Rev. James Putt, Th.M., pastor of the Fourth Christian Reformed
Church in Chicago, in his pamphlet on *Masonry,* says:

"The full name of the Masonic Order is 'Ancient and Accepted Freemasonry.' This leaves the impression that it dates back
many centuries. According to the *Encyclopedia Britannica,* it had
its inception not earlier than 1717 A.D. The degrees of the
Scottish Rite were set in order in 1762. In 1786 there were
some changes and regulations made. There are some degrees
in Masonry today that are supposed to be a continuation of orders
that existed already during the times of the Crusades, as for example, the Knights Templar. But these orders were not intro-
duced into Masonry until the beginning of the eighteenth century.

"The history of the Mystic Shrine to which all Masonic
degrees lead, tells us that it was established at Mecca, Arabia,
and later revived and instituted at Cairo, Egypt, with the purpose
of promoting, organizing, and perfecting the Arabian and Egyp-
tian Inquisition, in order to dispense justice and execute punishment upon criminals. When it was brought to this country, it
was placed in the hands of the Masons. This took place in the
early part of the eighteenth century."

(This scholarly pamphlet of thirty-one pages, with references and
bibliographies, is published by Zondervan Publishing House and is
very good.)

Again I say that the claim to antiquity made by Masonry is a false claim. High and leading Masons know that it is false. By claims of great age and sometimes of divine origin, Masonry seeks for itself an authority that it does not deserve, and by these false pretenses it catches the unlearned. And this claim to great age is such a swindle, so dishonest, that any Christian ought to be devoutly ashamed to have a part in it.

The lodges make great claim to benevolence, but generally that claim is unfounded. The lodges, in fact, support their own homes for aged Masons and their wives, and for the orphan children of Masons, it is true. At Arlington, Texas, is an Eastern Star home and a home for aged Masons. At Fort Worth, Texas, is the Masonic Orphans Home. But do these homes receive anyone who is old and poor, or does the orphanage receive any children who are needy and left without father or mother, etc.? Indeed they do not! They receive those whose way has been paid ahead of time. The lodges are simply big insurance organizations. People who enter them pay in enough for dues and fees to guarantee that they themselves will be cared for when necessary. Masons who keep their dues paid up and who carefully preserve their connection will be relieved when in distress. But remember that they have paid for that privilege. The care that Masonry gives to the aged, the poor, and the orphans, is no more than insurance companies all over the world do for those who have taken out insurance policies and paid the premiums. The boasted benevolence of the lodges, I say, is a swindle.

I am thinking just now of a Scottish Rite hospital for crippled children. There, I understand, crippled children are treated whether or not their parents are Masons. Well and good. We are glad for all the benevolence that they exercise toward those in trouble. I do know that *generally* the benevolence of the lodges is simply returning a part of the great amount paid in dues and fees, and that *generally* it is a selfish benevolence, never for the general public.

Certainly the benevolence of the lodges cannot compare with that of Roman Catholics in their many orphanages and schools and homes. I am not a Catholic, but I respect a sincere love for the poor and the destitute.

How different is the benevolence of the lodges from that commanded in the Bible.

Listen to what Jesus said:

"When thou makest a dinner or a supper, call not thy friends, nor thy brethren, neither thy kinsmen, nor thy rich neighbours; lest they also bid thee again, and a recompence be made thee.

But when thou makest a feast, call the poor, the maimed, the lame, the blind: And thou shalt be blessed; for they cannot recompense thee: for thou shalt be recompensed at the resurrection of the just" (Luke 14:12-14).

Let us compliment lodge men when they take care of their own widows and orphans and aged. Let us be glad about all the moral precepts which are sometimes taught in the lodges. Let us admit that many splendid men and women are in the lodges—many of them church people and preachers. But the "benevolence" of the lodges is not benevolence at all. In general it is simply a counterpart of the protection of commercial insurance companies. They take care of their own who have paid to be taken care of; they are certainly not in the class with the churches; and their spirit and works are not those of the Christian religion. (I speak of the lodges themselves, and not of individuals.) The boasted benevolence of the lodges is simply not benevolence, but is paying back a part of what is paid in dues and fees.

Sometimes lodge members have said that the lodges are the handmaidens of the church. But that is untrue, just as the claims of secret and unpublished knowledge, the claims to a great age, the claims to divine origins, the claims that ancient prophets were patrons of the lodges, are all untrue. And the falsity of those claims is such that Christians should be ashamed to take part in the swindle that is put over upon the ignorant when people are led into lodge membership. Lodges live by dishonest claims and are a swindle.

CHAPTER VIII

Lodge Oaths Not Binding on Christians: Should Be Renounced and Broken

When initiated into the Entered Apprentice degree, I was induced to swear that *"I will always hail, ever conceal and never reveal any of the secret arts, parts or points of the hidden mysteries of ancient Freemasonry, which have been heretofore, may at this time or shall at any future period be communicated to me as such...."* Yet, in this series of articles, I have solemnly and in the name of Christ renounced that oath; and here I do not hail, and I do not conceal the so-called secret arts and points of Masonry, but am rather helping to reveal them as a Christian duty laid upon me by my God and by the Scriptures and my conscience.

Ought a Christian who has been led into the lodges, or one who was in a lodge and later converted, count those oaths binding upon him? Ought he to abide by them? What ought a Christian to do if he has taken oaths which he comes to know are unchristian and wicked and contrary to the Bible? That is an honest question, and I will answer it earnestly and honestly, in the fear of God, and calling upon Him to help me do right about it.

It is my firm conviction, as it is the conviction of thousands of other earnest Christians, that a child of God who has been guilty of taking lodge oaths ought to renounce them and break them. I believe I can show you from the Bible and from reason that God Himself requires you to renounce those wicked oaths, and that you cannot keep them and please God.

Note the following reasons why a Christian should renounce his lodge oaths and count them null and void:

(1) Lodge oaths are exacted of men who have never been given a chance to know what they are ahead of time. The oaths are given, at least in most cases, and perhaps in all cases, a line at a time; and the candidate is never given a chance to meditate ahead of time. Had I known ahead of time the bloodthirsty oath required of me, I would never have entered a Masonic lodge to take the Entered Apprentice work. Multiplied thousands would not. Such a blind contract, into which one is compelled

to enter without an understanding of the terms of the contract, would not be binding in any court of law and is utterly unfair.

(2) Second, the oath is extorted on false pretenses. The candidate is solemnly assured that it will not conflict with his duty to his family, his country, nor his God, and that is not true. Literally tens of thousands of Christian men have found that the lodge oaths require them to neglect their families and keep secrets from their wives. Lodge oaths require candidates to bind themselves to conceal the crimes of fellow lodge members, usually excepting murder and treason, sometimes excepting not even those crimes. Lodge oaths would thwart justice and violate a man's duty, then, to his country. And since Jesus Christ and the Bible expressly commanded, "Swear not at all" (Matt. 5:34), and the inspired Apostle James commanded, "Above all things, my brethren, swear not" (Jas. 5:12), and the inspired Apostle Paul commanded, "Be ye not unequally yoked together with unbelievers" (II Cor. 6:14), then the lodge oath is a flagrant violation of any Christian's duty to God. I say any such oath, which is given under false pretenses, is not binding. No court in the land would regard it as binding. Any such contract would not be recognized by honorable men anywhere as binding between two men.

The oath is given under false pretenses in that the candidate is promised he will be given some great secrets not written down and not to be obtained otherwise. That promise is false, because again and again the material has been printed and circulated by tens of thousands of copies; and intelligent, reading, inquiring men and women can buy it and read it. To pretend that there are great mysteries and secret lessons in the lodges, and on that pretense require bloodcurdling oaths, is so dishonest that neither God nor government nor fair-minded men can hold a man to such an oath, so falsely obtained.

(3) Lodge oaths ought to be renounced and broken because it is impossible for a good man and a faithful Christian to keep these oaths. Consider what the oaths require:

(a) The candidate taking the oath is sworn to endorse the death penalty for himself and, in some cases, sworn to exact it of others. No good man, no faithful Christian man, can honestly keep an oath that binds him to murder or endorses murder.

(b) Some of the oaths certainly require the one who takes them to persecute and slander and harm those who may be called "traitors" to the lodge, to follow them as long as they live, count them as vagabonds, and hurt their good name. No really good man, no faithful Christian, can live up to such an oath.

(c) The oaths may require men to lie. For instance, one who swears: "always to hail, ever to conceal and never to reveal," binds himself to deceive. Can he "always hail" that which he learns is evil? Not honestly. Suppose that an earnest Christian does not intentionally reveal any of the so-called secrets of the lodges. But can he always honestly conceal them? Again and again I have known of cases where lodge members were asked the plain question whether or not certain oaths were part of the lodge obligations. Wives ask their husbands if it is true that in the lodges they are not to pray in the name of Christ, and if it is true that unconverted Jews are received on an equality with Christians, and if it is true that large amounts are spent for fees, etc. Men who are sworn to conceal such matters, then, must deceive. They must conceal the truth. They are sworn not to act nor talk as if the truth were true. For that reason, some lodge members will denounce this series of articles as lies and falsehoods. They are sworn to do so. They are sworn to conceal the truth. Can a good man, a faithful Christian, always conceal the truth when sometimes he must speak?

(d) The lodge oaths obligate lodge members to protect lodge criminals, to keep their secrets, to aid them in any business they have, to answer their cry of distress. To keep lodge oaths, one must sometimes be a poor citizen. Good men, really faithful Christian men, cannot keep such an oath.

(e) Lodge oaths bind lodge members to prefer lodge members to their brethren in Christ in the churches, to promote lodge members in business and in politics, and even to remember them in prayer, more than they obligate themselves to do for Christians not members of the lodges. Can really faithful Christians keep such oaths, preferring unconverted men, Christ-rejecting men, to their brethren in Christ? Certainly they cannot do that and please God.

I say that Christians ought to renounce and forsake their lodge oaths because good men, really faithful Christian men, cannot keep such oaths! It would be a sin to keep such oaths. It would be a righteous duty to break the oaths and renounce them.

(4) God's Word plainly requires a Christian to break a bad and sinful oath. The teaching of the Scripture is that if one swears to do either good or evil, but it is hid from him what he swears, then when

he knows of it, he should count himself guilty and confess it as a sin. Leviticus 5:4, 5 says:

"Or if a soul swear, pronouncing with his lips to do evil, or to do good, whatsoever it be that a man shall pronounce with an oath, and it be hid from him; when he knoweth of it, then he shall be guilty in one of these. And it shall be, when he shall be guilty in one of these things, that he shall confess that he hath sinned in that thing."

First, it is counted a sin to swear to a hidden obligation. Second, the man is guilty whether the oath he took was to do evil or to do good. And third, when he knows of it, he should feel his guilt and should confess his oath as a sin. The Old Testament Jew was also required to bring a trespass offering unto the Lord for this sin in swearing to something that was hid from him.

When a lodge member takes an oath to always hail, never to reveal and always to conceal things that he will learn about in the future, he is doing that which is plainly forbidden in the Bible. But when he later finds the thing he has sworn to is a sin, he should recognize that he has been guilty of a sin, and he should OPENLY CONFESS IT AS A SIN! Surely that expressly teaches that one should renounce a bad oath, and particularly should renounce any oath that is required concerning hidden things that later are to be revealed to him. God's Word thus requires a Christian to renounce wicked oaths, confess the sin in making them, and be bound by them no longer.

Some men have an idea that any oath or promise should always be kept. That is not the teaching of the Bible. If one makes a bad vow, God places restrictions about it; and when one discovers that the vow was not the proper one to make, he is released from that vow. For example, in Numbers, chapter 30, we are told that if a woman makes a vow to God and then later her husband, or her father if she is at home with her father, hears about the vow and feels it is not right, he has the right to make it void, and the woman is not to be held responsible for it. Vows are sacred, but in such a case when a woman would learn later that her judgment was not good, even in making a promise to God, she should abide by the husband's or father's decision; and God would not hold her accountable to fulfill the vow she made. Remember that this is true even about a good vow. How much more it would be true about a vow which one would afterwards learn was wicked and ought never to have been made! *The lodges are presumptuous and sinful in trying to make God Almighty enforce their wicked, unscriptural vows which are plainly rebuked by the Scriptures.* If a lodge member made a vow or swore an oath in good faith, then as long as he is convinced that the vow or oath was right, he should live up to it. But when he learns that it was a sin to make the vow or to swear the oath and finds that it is contrary to the will of God, then he is bound to renounce the vow or oath if he serves God.

Some who read this took oaths which you now know are wicked and that you ought not to have taken them. What shall you do about them? Listen again to the Word of God:

"He that covereth his sins shall not prosper: but whoso confesseth and forsaketh them shall have mercy."—Prov. 28:13.

God wants you to confess and forsake and renounce the wicked oaths that you took which no Christian has a right to take. Confession is for true Christians the condition for forgiveness.

"If we confess our sins, he is faithful and just to forgive us our sins, and to cleanse us from all unrighteousness."—I John 1:9.

We should sometimes confess such faults to some others, too, for God's Word says:

"Confess your faults one to another, and pray one for another, that ye may be healed."—Jas. 5:16.

The Bible requires one to renounce and confess false oaths, particularly oaths concerning hidden things. In fact, the Bible commands a Christian to confess and forsake sin as a condition of cleansing and forgivness for that sin. It is a Christian duty to renounce and quit and be free from lodge oaths.

(5) Logical examples prove one should not be bound by false oaths. For example, George Washington swore, "that I will be faithful and bear true allegiance to our most sovereign Lord, King George III, and him will defend to the utmost of my power against all conspiracies and attempts whatever that shall be made against his person, crown and dignity." George Washington took that oath of the Virginia Militia. (*Masonic Oaths Null and Void,* by Edmond Ronayne, page 173.) Later, George Washington, after earnest prayer, came to the solemn conviction that he ought to help the American colonies get their freedom from the wicked oppression of King George III. Do you believe that he was right to renounce an oath when he found that it was contrary to the will of God and righteousness? Certainly you do! Then how much more is it right for a Christian to renounce an oath which was obtained under false pretenses, one which is contrary to his duty to God and family and his country, after he finds in the Word of God clear command

that he should not have taken any such oath nor have yoked up with unbelievers!

In New Testament times, more than forty Jews "banded together, and bound themselves under a curse, saying that they would neither eat nor drink till they had killed Paul" (Acts 23:12, 13). They swore to kill Paul. Now, that was a wicked oath. If one of these conspirators had been converted and had become convinced of the awful wickedness of his oath, would it have been a sin for him to renounce the oath and break it? Manifestly not! Would he have been right to break that oath and refuse to kill Paul? Rather, to have broken the oath would have been his plain duty and to have kept it would have been an awful sin. And exactly so, when a Christian, a child of God, finds that he has wickedly sinned in taking oaths that are forbidden in the Word of God, then he ought to renounce those oaths and be bound by them no longer. To do otherwise would be a sin.

The Bible itself recognizes that vows may be rightly broken sometimes. For instance, when a man and woman marry, they take each other "till death do us part"; yet, for the sin of fornication or adultery the Saviour Himself plainly permitted divorce (Matt. 19:3-9).

King Herod swore to the dancing daughter of the wicked, adulterous queen Herodias that he would give her anything she asked, even to the half of his kingdom. Her mother hated John the Baptist for his plain talk against her sin and had the girl to ask for "the head of John the Baptist." Herod had the great preacher slain and presented his head on a platter. He committed this sin "for his oath's sake." Does any intelligent Christian think he did right? Rather, do you not know he should have broken any such wicked oath instead of murdering the man of whom Jesus said there was never a greater born of woman?

It is clearly a duty to break and renounce any wicked oath that binds one in sin. So every lodge member should renounce his wicked oath and confess it as a sin and be forgiven, and so stop adding his influence to the sins of the lodges which damn so many souls with their false religion.

I talked to a lost man once urging him to trust the Saviour. He was in the deepest distress of mind. When I pressed the matter upon him, finally he said that he could not do it, that he was under a sworn oath to kill a certain man. As I remember, he had sworn to his father on the father's deathbed that he would kill his father's enemy. He felt bound by that wicked oath and said that he could not be a Christian, of course, if he were going to murder that man, and yet he felt bound to do so.

I told him that according to the Bible it would be wicked to keep the oath, but that it would honor God to break it. He was wrong in the first place to take any such oath. Later when he saw that it was wrong, his plain duty was to renounce and break the oath which was ungodly and which God never did endorse nor approve. Just so, it is manifestly the plain duty of every man who has taken a sinful, wicked oath, contrary to the command of God, an oath that would lead him constantly into sin if he observed it—it is his plain duty, I say, to renounce and break that oath.

Thus, I have come to the conclusion to which God has led thousands of other Christians: Evangelist Charles G. Finney, then   President of Oberlin College; Elder Stearns, Baptist preacher who wrote *Light on Masonry;*Captain William Morgan who renounced Masonry and exposed its sinful secrets and sealed his testimony with his blood when he was murdered by Masons; Rev. Wendell P. Loveless, my neighbor at Wheaton, Illinois; Edmond Ronayne, and many others. It is your duty, Christian, not only to leave the lodges, but to confess your sin and forsake it.   You should admit your wrong and stop the bad influence which you have used for these unchristian institutions.

CHAPTER IX

"Wherefore Come Out from Among Them, and Be Ye Separate, Saith the Lord"

Let us return now to II Corinthians 6:14-18 and consider prayerfully the duty of a Christian who is a lodge member:

"Be ye not unequally yoked together with unbelievers: for what fellowship hath righteousness with unrighteousness? and what communion hath light with darkness? And what concord hath Christ with Belial? or what part hath he that believeth with an infidel? And what agreement hath the temple of God with idols? for ye are the temple of the living God; as God hath said, I will dwell in them, and walk in them; and I will be their God, and they shall be my people. Wherefore come out from among them, and be ye separate, saith the Lord, and touch not the unclean thing; and I will receive you, And will be a Father unto you, and ye shall be my sons and daughters, saith the Lord Almighty."—II Cor. 6:14-18.

God says come out from among the unconverted and unbelievers. God says break the yoke. God says be separate. Child of God, is it difficult for you to know what to do?

Ephesians 5:11, 12 says:

"And have no fellowship with the unfruitful works of darkness, but rather reprove them. For it is a shame even to speak of those things which are done of them in secret."

Don't walk in the counsel of the ungodly; don't stand in the way of sinners; don't sit in the seat of the scornful, dear child of God!

Have no fellowship with these works of darkness, the Lord commands.

The most spiritual and most trusted Christian leaders of the past and present have given their testimony against secret orders and lodges, and urged Christians who loved God to come out from among them and be separate. The great Moody Church in Chicago, of which Dr. Harry A. Ironside was long pastor, founded by D. L. Moody, and which had pastors like Drs. R. A. Torrey, Paul Rader, James M. Gray and P. W. Philpott in the past, requires one to renounce lodges and secret orders to be a member of that great church. The Cicero Bible Church, of which Rev. William McCarrell, long president of the Independent Fundamental Churches of America, is pastor, has the same stand. Wheaton College, an old independent Christian college at Wheaton, Illinois, had the same stand. Drs. Jonathan Blanchard and Charles A. Blanchard, great presidents of Wheaton, were widely known for their vigorous stand against lodges. In 1932, this author preached in the Chicago Gospel Tabernacle on the text "Be ye not unequally yoked together with unbelievers," and a trustee of Wheaton College immediately asked me to go and give that message in the college, which I did.

Here is what D. L. Moody said about secret orders:

"I do not see how any Christian, most of all a Christian minister, can go into these secret lodges with unbelievers. They say they can have more influence for good; but I say they can have more influence for good by staying out of them, and then reproving their evil deeds. Abraham had more influence for good in Sodom than Lot had. If twenty-five Christians go into a secret lodge with fifty who are not Christians, the fifty can vote anything they please, and the twenty-five will be partakers of their sins. *They are unequally yoked together with unbelievers.* 'But,' says some one, 'what do you say about these secret temperance orders?' *I say the same thing.* Do not evil that good may come. You can never reform anything by unequally yoking yourself with ungodly men. True reformers separate themselves from the world. 'But,' you say, 'you had one of them in your church.' So I had, but when I found out what it was I cleaned it out like a cage of unclean birds. They drew in a lot of young men of the church in the name of temperance, and then they got up a dance and kept them out till after twelve at night. I was a partaker of their sins, because I let them get into the church; but they *were cleaned out, and they never came back.* This idea of promoting temperance by yoking one's self up in that way with ungodly men is abominable. The most *abominable* meeting I ever attended was a temperance meeting in England. It was full of secret societies, and there was no Christianity about it. I felt as though I had got into Sodom, and got out as soon as I could. A man rescued from intemperance by a society not working on gospel principles gets filled with pride and boasts about reforming himself. Such a man is harder to save than a drunkard. 'But, Mr. Moody,' some say, 'if you talk that way you will drive all the members of secret societies out of your meetings and out of your churches.' But what if I did? Better men will take their places. Give them the truth anyway, and if they would rather leave their churches than their lodges, the sooner they get out of the churches the better. I would rather have ten members who are separated from the world than a thousand such members. Come out from the lodge. Better one with God than a thousand without Him. We must walk with God, and if only one or two go with us, it is all right. Do not let down the standard to suit men who love their secret lodges or have some darling sin they will not give up."

"Be ye not unequally yoked together with unbelievers: for what fellowship hath righteousness with unrighteousness? . . . or what part hath he that believeth with an infidel?

"Wherefore come out from among them, and be ye separate, saith the Lord."—II Cor. 6:14, 15, 17.

D. L. Moody was vigorous in his influence against secret orders. His great Christian Workers' Conferences, with leading preachers and Bible teachers from England and America, led many a preacher and student to forsake the secret orders. Nazarene churches forbid members to join the lodges. So do the Mennonites. So do many branches of the Lutheran churches. The Christian Reformed denomination has denounced the lodge also, and forbids members to join the lodge.

After the murder of William Morgan, it is estimated that 45,000 Masons quit Masonic lodges, leaving probably less than 10,000. More than 2,000 lodges were disbanded!

The great Evangelist Charles G. Finney, who won some 200,000 souls to Christ and then founded the Oberlin College of which he was long president, wrote a remarkable book on *The Character, Claims and Practical Workings of Freemasonry.* This great preacher, soul winner, educator, and writer gives proof so convincing and so plainly stated, and in such Christian spirit, that it is overwhelming.

The book, *Heresies Exposed,* compiled by William C. Irvine, editor of *The Indian Christian,* with introduction by Dr. Louis T. Talbot, long pastor of Church of the Open Door and president of the Bible Institute of Los Angeles, has gone through ten editions. Among other false cults exposed in this book is "Freemasonry." There is abundance of literature on the subject, written by earnest Christian men.

Notice this remarkable list of great Christian men and statesmen who have denounced the lodges and opposed them, particularly Masons: "John Wesley, Alexander Campbell, Daniel Webster, Wendell Phillips, Chief Justice Marshall, Charles Sumner, John Hancock, Horace Greeley, Joseph Cook, D. L. Moody, R. A. Torrey, Timothy Dwight, Chas. G. Finney and J. H. Fairchild (presidents of Oberlin College), Jonathan and Charles A. Blanchard (presidents of Wheaton College), John Adams, James Madison, Amos Wells, Simon Peter Long, James M. Gray." (See *Masonry* by James Putt, Th.M., Zondervan Publishing House.) In Princeton Theological Seminary, as in other institutions, courses in modern cults and false religions include an exposure of the false teachings of fraternal orders.

The lodges are organized. They threaten to boycott commercially, and to persecute and slander those who oppose the lodges. Many who have convictions against the lodges have no organization, no means of publication. Some are timid and fear to lose friends and position. But I tell you now, that the widespread sentiment of the most useful soul winners and many sincere Christians in the world is against the Christ-rejecting lodges, with their oath-bound yokes with unbelievers, their blasphemies, and their unchristian and antichristian false religion and their denial of blood redemption.

And do you love the lodges so much more than Christ that you fear to do right for Him if you lose a few friends?

I have thanked God many times for an earnest word spoken in a homiletics class by the saintly Dr. Jeff D. Ray at the Southwestern Theological Seminary at Fort Worth, Texas. He warned young preachers of the dangers of yoking up with unbelievers in the lodges.

Since the first of these articles appeared in *The Sword of the Lord,* I have received many letters on the question of the lodges, and to my surprise, without exception, they are praising God for such plain speech and telling again and again how the writers, after they were soundly converted, were led by the Holy Spirit to quit the lodges. Others tell how their fathers were lodge members, but the Holy Spirit led them away from such a sin. One Christian, in a letter, tells how Dr. R. K. Maiden, a Baptist preacher and editor, whispered to him at a Masonic funeral, saying, "George, listen for the name of Jesus Christ." The writer then tells how shocked he was that the name of Christ was never mentioned, and how surprised he was to hear the Masonic funeral service teaching salvation as the just reward of a pure and holy life! Another man, on fire for God, writes to say that when he was converted, God showed him who his brothers were. "Who is my BROTHER?" says Jesus. "He that heareth the words of my Father and doeth them." So he quit the lodges. Preachers write to encourage me. One man wrote to tell how a friend was converted reading the very first issue containing these articles. Many, many have written, asking for extra copies of these papers by ones and twos and by bundles. *I say that the sentiment of multiplied thousands of devout Christians is that no child of God has any business in the lodges.* And the Holy Spirit says, "Wherefore come out from among them, and be ye separate, saith the Lord, and touch not the unclean thing; And I will receive you, and will be a Father unto you, and ye shall be my sons and daughters, saith the Lord Almighty" (II Cor. 6:17, 18).

The late Dr. James M. Gray, then president of Moody Bible Institute, said in an address urging Christians to come out of the lodges and not yoke up with unbelievers in their counterfeit religion:

"In conclusion, I do not expect that anything I am saying will change the mind of any lodge member, but I sincerely hope to be instrumental under God in saving some young men, and especially students of the Christian ministry, from entanglement with what I consider to be a great delusion; to plead with them to separate themselves from the whole system, as I would plead with them about any other moral or spiritual counterfeit. I plead with them to separate themselves from it, because it is dishonoring to Jesus Christ; because it is hurtful to the truest interests of the soul; because it has the stamp of the dragon upon it.

"As my friend the late Dr. A. J. Gordon of Boston said, 'We become unavoidably and insensibly assimilated to that which most completely absorbs our time and attention.' One cannot be constantly mixed in secular society without unknowingly losing some of his interest in the divine society of God and of angels, where he belongs by his new birth. Our citizenship is in heaven, my Christian brothers, and we ought to be careful where we are living and refuse to be attracted by any system which is a rival of the blood-bought church of the Redeemer."

Stephen Merritt, as mentioned earlier in this book, was a Mason, the Master of the biggest lodge in New York, years ago. He wrote the thrilling true experience of Samuel Morris, a heathen African boy who was led to come to America to learn about the Holy Spirit from Stephen

Merritt. Mr. Merritt died in 1917, but his testimony about how he was led to renounce the lodge still lives.

Speaking at a convention of the National Christian Association at Utica, New York, he told how a lodge member who was thought to be dying called for him and reproached him. Said the stricken man, "You told me then that it was all right if I was an upright man, and obeyed the precepts of the lodge, but I am leaning on a broken reed; and now I am dying without God. I lay this to your charge, Worshipful Master. I leaned on you and now I am dying." That broke Merritt's heart, and he never got away from it. The stricken Mason got well and was converted and urged Merritt to get out of the lodge. Now let this great Christian layman tell his own story:

"About a month ago there was a precious meeting in the Tabernacle with our poor people. There came a great hush upon the congregation. The Holy Spirit was there in power, as we talked of Him. It was a solemn time. I felt subdued and close to God, and said, 'I am Thine: I am altogether Thine, Lord.' But the Holy Ghost said, 'THAT WEDGE OF GOLD!' I said, 'All is thine. There is nothing between me and Thee.' He only said, 'THAT WEDGE OF GOLD!' Then I remembered under the floor of my tent, oh, I had hidden a wedge of gold! I had kept a beautiful jewel which was a present from the lodge and worth $250 or more, made of gold, with a diamond suspended in it.

* * *

"I wrote a letter to the Temple Lodge No. 203, and told them God had told me to sever all connection with Masonry forever. Then I enclosed the jewel and sent it. The members of the lodge came to talk with me. I was told it would ruin my business; that it would hurt me in a thousand ways. 'Don't break off,' they pleaded. They wanted me to keep the jewel. They said, 'We don't know what to do with it.' I told them I would not give it house-room. They might melt it up and give it to the poor, if they wanted to. It was a wedge of gold in my tent and I would have it there no longer.

"This was only about a month ago. It was the last link that bound me to the world. Now I am free. I will not have anything between Jesus and my soul. In this convention I am standing for the first time a free man! For whom the Son makes free, he is free indeed. I never had such a blessed deliverance.

"I thank God the seal of the Spirit is on me; that I am walking in the light. They used to lead me about blindfolded, in the lodge.

It was the blind leading the blind into the ditch. We must get out of that mire, and put our feet on the solid foundation, the Rock Christ Jesus. There only are we safe."

Christian, I have urged upon you the solemn duty to break the yoke that binds you in secret orders, and to come out from among them and please God. You, too, may have the sweet peace of God. Christ Himself will make up to you all you lose in friends and all you lose in business. Do not be afraid to step out in faith. God has said of wisdom, that "her ways are ways of pleasantness, and all her paths are peace" (Prov. 3:17). No one ever lost by doing what God said. Better yet, Jesus said, "Take my yoke upon you, and learn of me; for I am meek and lowly in heart: and ye shall find rest unto your souls. For my yoke is easy, and my burden is light" (Matt. 11:29, 30). And may God give you joy in your heart; may the way be clear between you and God when you pray; and may you have power from Heaven on your testimony to win unconverted, dying men to trust the Lord Jesus Christ and love Him and serve Him!

If some person reads this booklet who does not know for sure that he or she is a child of God, then let me urge upon you that you make sure today. Jesus Christ died to save sinners—sinners, mind you, not good people! For we are all sinners, and God's only way of saving sinners is to have them trust in Jesus Christ and be cleansed by His atoning blood. Do not look upon the filthy garments of your righteousness. God will have none of them! Do not count upon church membership, nor lodge membership, nor morality. The only hope for a sinner is that Christ died for sinners. Put your trust in Him today and be saved!